HAUNTED
LIVERPOOL 5

For Skelly, Duchess and Butch

© Tom Slemen 2001

Edited by Claire Walker
Published by The Bluecoat Press, Liverpool
Book design by March Design, Liverpool
Front cover illustration and photograph by Angela Mounsey
Printed by D2P, Llandudno

ISBN 1 872568 80 7

Tom Slemen

HAUNTED
LIVERPOOL 5

The Bluecoat Press

Contents

Introduction

Where are we? Who are we? Why are we here? Simple questions which defy simple answers and have taxed mankind for thousands of years. I had a good friend many years ago, when I was about eight or nine, who used to drive adults up the wall with such apparently innocent questions.

"Why is the grass green?" he asked his father one day as he was playing in the garden.

His father wracked his brains for a moment, before recalling one of the few things he vaguely remembered from botany lessons at school: chlorophyll, the green pigment present in most plants.

"Chlorophyll, son; that makes the grass look green," his father stated, somewhat uncertainly.

"Oh I know that, but why is it green?" his son persisted haughtily.

"It just is, accept it," his father retorted with some impatience.

"And why is the sky blue?" his inquisitive son continued, squinting his eyes at the heavenly azure canopy over Edge Hill.

"Why don't you go and watch the telly?" his ruffled father suggested, as he returned to studying the racing section of his newspaper, trying to soak up some of the afternoon sun.

Even at school, my pal was just as persistent with his incessant questioning, his thirst for knowledge seemingly unquenchable. He once stopped the teacher in the middle of a science lesson:

"Sir, when you switch the light off, where do all the light rays go?"

"They fly off at the speed of light," was the teacher's curt explanation.

"But sir, you said light waves bounce off objects, so how do they ever manage to leave the room?"

"Because light is made of photons and we now know that light is not made up of waves," the teacher sighed.

"Who's 'we', sir?" some joker asked, as my classmate proceeded to reason.

"But, sir, I thought you said photons bounce off objects, so how do they ever get out of a closed room?"

At this stage the teacher became visibly irritated by his constant questioning.

"Enough nonsense!" he briskly announced.

I remember thinking that my friend was right to ask his questions, even though he gave me many sleepless nights with his conundrums. On one particularly tricky occasion, he took hold of my football and held it up in the air.

"Imagine this ball is the size of a planet and made of solid steel, and it has been travelling across space for millions of light years. Now, imagine if nothing in the universe could stop it, right?"

I blinked and nodded lamely and my associate continued his hypothesising.

"Right, now imagine that fence over there is a steel wall, and nothing in the universe can move it, even anti-matter bombs bounce off it. Now, what happens if the steel planet goes in that direction?"

I was stuck for words. My friend held the football out as if it was an unexploded bomb, and paced his way dramatically towards the fence saying:

"What happens when the thing that can't be stopped, meets the thing that can't be moved?"

"The steel planet goes through the wall?" was my feeble suggestion.

"No, the wall can't budge, even its atoms can't move apart to let the steel planet through." His tone became more serious, as he held the football just inches away from the fence. Then he continued, "… and the steel planet can't bounce off, because it's unstoppable and to reverse, it would have to stop first."

"Okay, I give up. What happens?" I asked in exasperation, thinking he would finally put me out of my misery.

"I don't know. I'll know one day though!" he shrugged.

Well, when I last saw my friend, he was desperately trying to steer a shopping trolley with a dodgy wheel in Tescos, as his kids persecuted him into buying cereal boxes containing Pokemon cards. On recognising him, I asked if he had yet solved 'the thing that can't be stopped meets the thing that can't be moved' puzzle. He confessed with a deep laugh that he had made no progress whatsoever, but as he made his way to the check out after our quick reunion, I heard him repeat the riddle to his children to shut them up!

It is strange how, with age, we lose the ability to question reality and our senses. This is exactly what leads me back to the original three seemingly simplistic questions I posed at the beginning of this introduction: where are we? who are we? and why are we here?

Where are we? Well, it is obvious we are 'here', but where exactly is here? Let us assume it is Liverpool. Now, Liverpool is identified and located by longitude and latitude on a globe we call the Earth, but just where is Earth? We know it is in the Solar System, which is in a spiral galaxy called the Milky Way, but we do not know where precisely that is. So, the truth of the matter is, we do not really know where we are in space or time. So let us explore this rudimentary ignorance a little further.

Within the unimaginable depths of the universe, there is a small family of worlds circling around a star we call the Sun; it is just a single star among the billions upon billions that are shining in the cosmos. Against the awesome backdrop of the infinite blackness of space, our world is just another planet; nothing more than an insignificant speck on the cosmological scale of things, but it is our home and, as of yet, we have found no other planets which are remotely like Earth.

The history of our world remains a story that is still largely incomplete. Just a few centuries ago, the most learned historians knew virtually nothing about events beyond three thousand years ago. These students of the past had a surplus of legends about the origin of man and his world, but the fables and myths were seemingly at variance with the fossilised bones of dinosaurs and ape-like beings. These archeological finds clashed severely with the beliefs and religions of people who took the Hebrew Bible's account of Genesis as an authentic history of the world. If prehistoric monsters roamed the Earth in the past, why were they not mentioned in the *Book of Genesis*? The halcyon tales of the Garden of Eden only mention Adam and Eve; there is no reference to the now-extinct races such as the Neanderthals, the Cro Magnon people and other sub-human anthropoids.

Despite the conflicting evidence of the fossil records, the Church attempted to circumvent the problem by seriously asserting that the Devil had maliciously fabricated the fossils of ancient plants and animals and had planted them in rocks to disprove the Biblical scriptures. In fact, by meticulous analysis of the *Book of Genesis*, the Archbishop of Armagh, James Usher (1581-1656) even came to the conclusion that God had created the world at 9am on October 23, 4004 BC! This claim is of course utter nonsense, which leads on to another unsettling truth: we cannot even be certain that we really know what time it is. You may glance at your watch and say, "We do know what time it is; it's 7.40pm". But compare it to someone else's watch and your timepiece will be seconds, possibly even minutes, ahead or behind. Furthermore, it is a different time all over the world because of the various time zones. Not only that, but when the first clocks were made, someone, somewhere had to say: "Okay, it is now officially the beginning of clock time and exactly noon."

However, when the first clocks came into use, the time varied greatly from village to village, because there were no radio signals to enable people to synchronise their clocks. But now that we have radio signals, no one is totally sure what time it is, because even the most reliable clocks in the world, the atomic clocks, are not one hundred per cent accurate. Even if they were, the time of day is just an abstract concept with no reality whatsoever. When the clocks are turned back an hour, or put forward in the spring, we simply accept it because it is convenient. We know very well we cannot physically advance time or set it back an hour, we are merely adjusting 'clock time', rather than real time. To know the real time we would have to know when time began, and it certainly did not begin as recently as 9am on 23 October 4004 BC as James Usher claimed! These are thought-provoking notions.

So we have established that we do not actually know where we are in space or time. I wonder if we will have better luck answering the second question: Who are we? As you are reading this you are probably thinking, "I know who I am. I am 'me'," but can you be more specific? because we all personally call ourselves 'me'. Saying that you are John Smith will not resolve this question either, as that is just the name that someone else gave you. All the philosophers and mystics have had a crack at this one. Descartes developed the notion of 'Cogito ergo sum' (I think, therefore I am) but he never explained what the 'I' actually was. Freud took things further when he identified the 'I' as the 'ego', but he was just putting a label on something he could not specifically fathom. The Indian mystics talk about 'finding yourself' and 'knowing yourself' but they have been saying that for centuries and they do not seem to be able to define exactly what the 'I' is either. Neurologists have even taken apart the human brain to investigate the seat of consciousness, or the 'I', but even they cannot pin down a fixed definition. In a nutshell then, it would seem that we don't even know who we are!

So then, why are we here? This third question has given philosophers a real headache. The Christians say we are here basically as a test for the life to come. 'Life is just an exam' John Lennon once said, but do we really honestly know if there is a purpose behind our existence? Are we here simply because we were conceived, or are we part of some Grand master plan, some metaphysical scheme beyond human understanding? The truth is that no one really knows, but many cults and religions claim to know the answer.

There is a tale in this book about a Victorian man who was so desperate to know what the 'afterlife' was like, that he employed a doctor to stop his heart momentarily so that he could have what we now know as a 'near death encounter'. When he returned to life, which was more by luck than by medical expertise, the Lazarus-like man believed he had been shown, by a godly entity, the ultimate answer concerning human existence. When the man communicated this knowledge to the living, the effects were catastrophic. Whether this was all hysteria is still unknown, but it makes you wonder doesn't it?

Even Winston Churchill once dreamt that he had learned the 'ultimate answer to the universe'. Apparently, he woke during the night and quickly wrote this answer down in a notebook on his bedside table. The next morning, when he awoke, he vaguely remembered the strange dream and grabbed at the notebook from the table near his bed to read the special 'answer' he had received from the enlightening dream. The single sentence read only this: 'The Whole is pervaded with the smell of turpentine'.

Apparently, Churchill shook his head in utter dismay. He had been almost certain that he had received a great truth in his dream the night before. Maybe he had, by mistake, and perhaps something replaced 'the ultimate answer' he had scribbled down with the nonsensical sentence about turps …

So many grey areas of unknowing surround us on all sides. We do not really know where we are, we do not know who we are and we have no real idea why we are here, yet people buy books like this one because they love the mystery of it all. Reader, your life is a major mystery, and it makes the stories you are holding before you simply pale into insignificance. I hope you enjoy the following tales anyway, even if they only distract you for a while from pondering upon the enigma of your own existence.

Tom Slemen

The Witche's Rede

I have had a lot of enquiries about the so-called 'Witche's Rede', a sort of creed in rhyme used by Wiccans to guide them and remind them of the ways of the Craft. This is it:

Bide the Wiccan Law ye must,
In perfect love, in perfect trust,
Live and let live,
Fairly take and fairly give.
Cast the circle thrice about,
To keep the evil spirits out.
To bind the spell every time,
Let the spell be spake in rhyme.
Soft of eye, light of touch,
Speak little, listen much.
Deosil go by waxing moon,
Chaning out the Witche's Rune.
Widdershins go by waning moon,
Chanting out the baneful rune,
When the lady's moon is new,
Kiss the hand to her, times two.
When the moon rides at her peak,
Then your heart's desire seek.
Heed the north wind's mighty gale,
Lock the door and drop the sail.
When the wind comes from the south,
Love will kiss thee on the mouth.
When the wind blows from the west,
Departed souls will have no rest.
When the wind blows from the east,
Expect the new and set the feast.
Nine woods in the cauldron go,
Burn them fast and blow them slow.
Elder be the lady's tree,
By the lady, blessed be.
Where rippling waters go,
Cast a stone and truth you'll know.
When ye have a true need,
Hearken not to others' greed.
With a fool no season spend,
Lest ye be counted as his friend.
Merry ye meet and merry ye part,
Bright the cheeks and warm the heart.
Mind the threefold law you should,
Three times bad and three times good.
When misfortune is enow,
Wear the blue star on thy brow.
True in love ever be,
Lest thy lover's false to thee.
Eight words in the Wiccan Rede fulfill:
An ye harm none, do what ye will.

Mysteries Explained

I have learned from personal experience that not all ghosts are as ghostly as they first seem, once you've done a bit of delving. I once went to a house where an elderly man reported seeing a spooky white figure from his window. Upon glancing out of the window I saw that the 'ghost' was in actual fact just a white shirt hanging upon a garden washing line about three hundred yards away! When I explained to the old man that it was only a shirt, he smiled with embarrassment and remarked, "And I thought it was a ghostie waving to me".

Take Five

On that very note, the specific sightings of a deceased woman would have been taken as proof of ghostly activity, had the circumstances of the following bizarre tale not become fully known. In 1908, a Hungarian man named Abel Varga came to Liverpool. About a year after his arrival, he met and soon married, a young Liverpool woman named Myrna. The seemingly contented couple settled down into married life in a house on Bloom Street, close to Canning Street.

In 1910, just a few years into their cosy new life together, Myrna tragically died from breast cancer, leaving the distraught Mr Varga visibly beside himself with grief. His neighbours did not know him too well, as he and Myrna had very much kept themselves to themselves. So after the premature death, nobody was sure how to approach the lonely widow to offer some support at such a terrible time. It was during the following weeks that something quite strange took place.

At half past midnight, Mary Hilditch, who lived facing Mr Varga, was about to close her bedroom curtains. As she leant across the dark window to do so, she distinctly saw the late Mrs Varga appear at the bedroom window of Varga's house. It was clearly Myrna, and the bemused neighbour could vividly see the dead woman's face, as she too was stretching to draw her curtains. Mrs Hilditch turned pale and stood back in disbelief, before dashing into the next room to tell her husband, William. He saw the fearful expression in his wife's eyes and calmly followed her back to the bedroom window. He leant in close and looked over at the house as well, but he could see nothing. He reassured his wife that she must have been mistaken and that she was just weary, encouraging her to get some rest. Nothing more was said of the confusing sighting.

However, a week later, Mr Hilditch and his wife both caught a glimpse of Myrna as she peeped out from behind the same curtains. It was undoubtedly Mr Varga's deceased wife, and Mary and William Hilditch gasped, making the sign of the cross as they both stood aghast. They were seeing a ghost and there was no other explanation, at least that was what they thought.

Mr Varga later bumped into Mrs Hilditch, who chose not to mention the ghostly visions she had seen of his wife. Instead, she carefully enquired about how he was coping with the terrible loss. Varga exhaled very slowly, and with a fixed stare, he admitted that he was just about managing. His eyes flickered nervously as he went on to explain that he was intending to move away soon, because the house held too many sad memories of Myrna in the later stages of her terminal illness. Varga looked sorrowful as he quietly explained that he was making plans to move on to a new house in Aigburth.

Several days later, Mrs Hilditch sat comfortably in her front room quietly reading. The peacefulness of the rainy afternoon was starkly interrupted by the sound of raised voices nearby. The shouting grew louder, provoking Mrs Hilditch to go and see what the disturbance was. A blazing row in Bloom Street had caused most of the neighbourhood to step outside their doors and take a look. The sight was something to behold, for there, before the inquisitive neighbours, stood Mr Varga and his supposedly dead wife, Myrna. The couple were in the middle of a heated argument on the pavement right outside their home. Myrna clutched a large packing case, which was slipping from her grasp, as her other hand pounded her husband.

It was not long before the police were called, but when they arrived, Mr Varga was suddenly nowhere to be seen. Myrna broke down emotionally, shouting that she was not Myrna at all. She sobbed that it was true that Myrna was dead, and through choked tears she went on to explain that she was actually Myrna's twin sister, Mary. It transpired that the elusive Abel Varga had married both sisters, who had consented to a bizarre and bigamous marital arrangement. The twins had both fallen for the handsome Hungarian and had been married in two different churches, under two different names. And so the unbelievable truth began to be unravelled. Apparently, only recently Mary had found out that her husband actually had three other wives in Hungary and France! Although the ghostly mystery was tidied up, allowing Mrs Hilditch to sleep easier at night, the bigamist Abel Varga was never heard of again.

The Gruesome Snowman

On 21 December 1857, Joan Ringer, a farmer's daughter, plodded through the deep snow, collecting firewood near Scarth Hill in Ormskirk. As the pretty 16-year-old struggled with her burdensome load of wood, she felt a hand grab her from behind. Terrified, she dropped the wood from her arms and turned around to face an aggressive-looking middle-aged man. Immediately aware that she was in terrible danger, she tried to break free and run back home, but the stranger just leered at her without uttering a word and blocked her path. The area was completely deserted and the heavy blanket of snow made it appear even more so. Joan shuddered, conscious that she had no chance of escape as the villainous attacker proceeded to brutally assault her. When it was all over, she lay trembling, helpless and half naked in the snow. Her wicked assailant then proceeded to produce a knife and in a detached tone he described how he was going to finish her off, seeming to take a great delight in watching the teenaged girl as she whimpered quietly but uncontrollably, so choked that she could not even utter a scream.

The only sound that interrupted the awful scene was the distant barking of a dog. Over on the far side of the field, Joan's father and brother were trudging through the deep snow to give her a hand with the wood. Suspicious of the male figure they could see on their land, and unable to see Joan, who was still hunched up in the snow, they tried to increase their pace but were impeded by the thick snow which was piled high in deep drifts. However, the attacker spotted them coming and turned to Joan with a snarl.

"I'll be back for you!" he hissed savagely through gritted teeth, his face purple with thwarted rage.

Then he turned and fled into the nearby wood.

Joan's father and brother saw him vanish and quickened their pace still further, falling over themselves in the snow as they struggled to reach the spot. When they finally came upon the pathetic, half-naked figure of Joan they were devastated. They quickly picked her up and covering her, they gently helped her back to the farmhouse. The farmer was enraged by what had happened to his daughter and tried to trace the tracks of the villain in the snow. However, his attempts were futile, as the snow had begun to melt in the middle of the forest, where it had dripped off the branches in the wintry sunshine and the tracks were gradually fading away.

That Christmas Day, a raging two-day blizzard finally ended, leaving a fresh coating of snow over the fields around the farm. Joan, her brother, and a cousin from Aughton, wandered across the virginal snow, revelling in the beauty of the magical landscape. Joan was bravely trying to overcome her ordeal as much as she could, and meekly joined in as they played, throwing snowballs at each other and sledging down a local hill. Presently they decided to build a snowman. They plodded their way across the snow-blanketed field, littered with old tools from the farm, whose forms had been obliterated by the snow drifts, and settled on a suitable spot. The three of them were soon engrossed in their task when, all of a sudden, Joan looked up and spotted a large snowman that somebody had already made in a nearby field.

The three teenagers dropped what they were doing and charged towards it. In all the fun, Joan had temporarily forgotten her recent experience and she led the way, gently giggling out loud as she ran straight at the snowman with a pitchfork, impaling it on the sharp prongs. She was surprised when the pitchfork jarred awkwardly as it hit the snowman's body: it didn't feel like compacted snow. The so-called snowman toppled over and red stains began to seep slowly through its snowy body; it was not a snowman at all, but a corpse, whose outline, like everything else in the frozen landscape, had been enlarged and softened by the recent snow. Joan screamed and almost fainted at the horrific reality. Her brother and cousin tried to reassure her as they leant over the snowy figure to take a closer look.

It certainly seemed to be the body of a man under the coating of ice and snow. The three were overcome with terror and ran home as fast as their legs would carry them to summon Farmer Ringer and contact the police. Joan's father was still reeling from the attack on his daughter a few days earlier and anxiously followed the three youngsters into the snow-covered field. When he reached the frozen corpse, he wiped the snow from its face. Joan looked on and was horror-stricken to find that it was the face of the man who had attacked her near Scarth Hill. The villain even had the knife on him with which he had threatened Joan, tucked away in a special leather sheath on his belt.

Subsequently, the body was identified as that of Mr George Eaves, by his younger brother, William. William Eaves informed the police that the last time he had seen his brother alive had been on Christmas Eve, when he had left their cottage in a drunken state, declaring in a slurred voice that he had unfinished business to attend to. It seems that George Eaves had probably been going to fulfil his promise of finishing Joan off, but in the freak, sub zero blizzard, he had been literally frozen in his tracks and had died from exposure as a result. After that grisly Christmas, Joan Ringer always shuddered whenever she saw a snowman.

A Kept Woman

This is a particularly weird story. In 1860 at Bevington Bush in Liverpool, a 50-year-old Lancashire man called Samuel Cadwalladr purchased a small cottage. Cadwalladr travelled all the way from his condemned, crumbling old house near what is now Thatto Heath, and literally arrived overnight in an old horse-drawn cart. Neighbours heard him steal into Bevington Bush at around four o'clock in the morning, and discussed amongst themselves that it seemed a strange and unearthly hour in which to move into a new residence. An old local man named James Allen was a light sleeper, and on hearing the disturbance he looked out of his window and saw Cadwalladr hauling his furniture and boxes off the cart. Single-handedly he struggled to carry them into the house. Mr Allen also heard Cadwalladr's voice being raised during what seemed to be a heated argument with his wife, whose name he later found out was Gryzmelda.

On the following morning, Samuel Cadwalladr went to the local shops and filled a basket with general groceries. He kept consulting a list which he clasped in his hand as he muttered to himself the words, "I cannot read what she writes". The shopkeeper surmised that Cadwalladr's wife had written out the shopping list.

The inexplicable thing was that no one ever saw Mrs Cadwalladr. Wild, extravagant rumours flew through Bevington Bush that Gryzmelda was a cripple with no legs, that she was someone else's wife, or that she was really his sister. The local residents were eager to find out why she was such a secretive figure. One neighbour called at the house carrying a large meat and potato pie which she had made for the Cadwalladrs as a kind gesture, but Samuel Cadwalladr just snatched the pie from her hands and closed the door in her face, without so much of a thank you. Another neighbour, who had noticed a gap at the bottom of the Cadwalladrs' front door, was so intrigued by the odd couple, that he crouched down on his stomach and tried to peep into the mysterious house. As he screwed up his eye to peer in, he could just about make out Samuel Cadwalladr waving his finger at someone as he argued, but the other person was just out of sight.

One night, a contingent of nosy neighbours gathered outside the cottage and watched the moving silhouette of Samuel Cadwalladr upon the curtains. They could see the shadows of Samuel holding his wife as he waltzed about the room after drinking his nightly pot of ale. The gossips were a little more contented now that they had at least caught a glimpse of the hidden woman's silhouette.

Then, one afternoon, Samuel Cadwalladr became ill and staggered out into the street in desperate pain. Neighbours went to fetch a Dr Mickledy, who immediately recognised the symptoms of a fever in in his patient. The doctor had the delirious Cadwalladr carried into his house and put to bed. The two neighbours who carried him into the tiny cottage, Mr Allen and Mr Cross, noticed that the elusive Mrs Cadwalladr was still nowhere to be seen.

As the two curious men searched the room with their eyes, they both noticed an old trunk which sat half open. As Dr Mickledy was attending Mr Cadwalladr, Mr Allen tipped open the ageing trunk. To his horror, he saw that it contained the mummified body of a woman. Her head was just a wrinkled skull, but her long red hair was still intact. The vision was grotesque, as the corpse's eyesockets were empty and the nose had totally collapsed. The most macabre thing about the corpse was the way in which the elbows and knees were connected. The limbs had been sawn through at the joints and dipped in tar. The elbows were attached to the upper arms with metal rings, and the kneecaps were joined in the same way. The corpse looked like a full size female doll.

When Cadwalladr recovered from the fever he made a hideous confession. He broke down as he explained that his wife had been a harridan who henpecked him and continually criticised him when they had failed to conceive after years of trying. After she had died of natural causes, Samuel Cadwalladr's sanity wavered. In a distorted attempt at revenge, as well as a reaction to the severe loneliness he experienced, he dug up her body one desperate night. After keeping the rotting corpse for a few days, he proceeded to mummify her remains by cutting off her arms and legs and rejoining them with metal rings.

In his rather unbalanced state, Cadwalladr would then periodically take the body out of the old trunk and treat it as if it were alive; this included having blazing rows with it, where Cadwalladr had the chance to release all his pent up anger from the unhappy marriage. The rows were always one-sided of course. At more sentimental moments, the deranged husband would seek comfort from his wife's remains and even dance with the corpse, as the neighbours had witnessed. This distressing charade had gone on for ten years.

Needless to say, after his ghastly secret had been revealed, Samuel Cadwalladr was soon committed to a lunatic asylum and Gryzmelda was given an appropriate, and final, burial.

Marriage Put on Hold

This is not a ghost story, but it certainly tells of a strange series of events. In 1914, a young Birkenhead man named Robert Wesley joined up with the Queen's Own Cameron Highlanders Machine Gun Corps. He had been married to his wife Maggie for just one year, and although they planned a family in the future, they did not yet have any children. Maggie bade him a tearful farewell as he went on his way, and soon Robert Wesley was fighting the Germans in France.

In the heart of battle, about a year after his departure from his hometown, Robert Wesley was placed at Chapel Hill in Hendicourt, when a thick fog enveloped the battlefields of France. From deep within the swirling mists, the Germans suddenly advanced. Wesley and his comrades, Vickers guns and all, were immediately captured and taken prisoner. During the traumatic experience, as the rest of the German troops were breaking through the British front lines, a piece of shrapnel from an exploding shell ripped out Robert Wesley's left eye. He was treated by the Germans, but kept as a prisoner of war until he was repatriated after the Armistice.

Robert Wesley returned to England to find his home and its surroundings unfamiliar. A strange family was now living in his Birkenhead residence, and his wife Maggie was no longer there. On leaving the premises with a heavy heart, Wesley passed some neighbours who were obviously completely shocked to see him. It soon came to light that the War Office had contacted Maggie Wesley a few years back to inform her that her husband had been killed in action, sadly a fairly common error. Wesley was deeply crushed as the neighbour broke the news to him that Maggie, in an attempt to rebuild her devastated life, had recently been courting a Liverpool man. She informed her old neighbour that Maggie's new romantic interest was called George Pilgrim, who was a local man living just off Scotland Road. Apparently the couple was due to marry in a week's time.

Wesley's sadness turned to fury and he immediately boarded the ferry to Liverpool to seek out his wife. As he sat down and tried to come to terms with the awful circumstances, doubt crept crept into his mind. Here he was a stranger, and an unattractive one at that, who had lost his eye in the war and now wore a patch. As these dismal thoughts buzzed through his mind, the poor man gradually lost his confidence and turned back, downhearted and dismayed.

He stayed temporarily with a friend in Vauxhall Road, who urged the distraught veteran to get back in touch with his wife. But Wesley remained reluctant, he was still devastated, and explained that he did not think he could bear to see her again now that he was disfigured. Undeterred, his concerned friend discovered that the wedding was to take place at St Anthony's church on Scotland Road that Thursday morning; Robert Wesley finally allowed himself to be persuaded to go, although he was not convinced of the wisdom of the decision. He stood at the back of the church and watched the wedding service. He smiled gently when he saw Maggie; she looked radiantly happy as she beamed broadly at her husband-to-be, surrounded by their friends and family.

At the stage of the ceremony when the priest asked if anyone present had any objections to the marriage, Robert Wesley felt his throat close up tightly with bitter sadness. After the service, he lingered nearby among the crowds to watch the newly-weds being showered with confetti. He knew that he could not compete with the man Maggie now loved and he strolled away, resigned to the fact he was to live a life of misery and solitude. From that day onwards, he lost interest in life, finding his only comfort was to hit the bottle.

Some 27 years later, in 1945, Robert Wesley was walking up Renshaw Street in Liverpool, when he bumped into Maggie as she came out of a shop. She did not know him at first, he was wearing his eye patch and his hair by now was a silvery grey, but she recognised his voice when he timidly asked, "Maggie, is it you?" The two stood there in startled silence. Maggie went completely weak at the sight of her supposedly deceased husband. To calm her shock, they went into a nearby café, where Robert Wesley could not help but tell her everything about why he had stayed in the shadows. Maggie was exasperated as she told him that she had never stopped thinking about him. She insisted that she would have loved him no matter what. As the two affectionately talked on, just as if they had never been apart, it transpired that George Pilgrim had turned out to be a wife beater and a drunk. The brute had died just five years after their terrible marriage.

As they gradually saw more and more of each other, George and Maggie decided to explain their unusual predicament to a local priest, who agreed to renew their wedding vows. The couple were never again parted, even to the extent that, when Robert died in 1967, Maggie followed close behind her husband and died just two days afterwards.

Amazing Coincidence

The following story recounts a remarkable coincidence that took place in 1926. That March, a 39-year-old Liverpool woman named Julia Rumbelow told her husband, Howard, that her Auntie Lily in Bethnal Green in London had been taken seriously ill. She explained that on hearing the news she had booked a week off work to go and visit her sick aunt.

Howard was a very laid back character and on hearing his wife's sudden plans, he just shrugged and nodded. The eleven-year-long marriage had become very stale; Julia had recently complained to friends at work that she felt that, in many ways, Howard was a complete stranger to her. She had only met his brother once at their wedding and had never met any other members of his family. Since Howard never mentioned them, she knew nothing about them. On top of that, Howard was not a socialiser, and the couple led a fairly isolated life. Julia was clearly unhappy in the stagnant relationship.

So, in reality, Julia Rumbelow was actually on her way to London to meet with 25-year-old Adam Jones, an office clerk she had recently met. Her Auntie Lily was not sick at all, it was just an excuse to spend time with her lover at a hotel a long way from home. After a hedonistic week of going out on the town, Adam treated Julia to a beautiful mink coat. With a passionate farewell embrace, the couple parted, whispering promises of another secret rendezvous in the near future. On her return to Liverpool, Julia realised that she would have to hide the luxurious gift, as it was evidence of her sins. Thinking quickly, she bought some brown paper and string and wrapped up the mink coat. She paid a few pence to leave the parcel at the luggage counter in Lime Street Station and made her way home.

Once she had sufficiently composed herself, Julia offered her husband the feeble excuse that she had found a left luggage ticket on the station platform and told him that she was considering claiming it. Suddenly, Howard jumped up and announced that he was just about to go into town. Pulling on his coat, he grabbed the ticket from her hand before she could say anything and said that he would collect whatever it was for her. Relieved that he had accepted her story and confident that her guilty secret was safe, Julia slowly started to relax and unpack.

Howard Rumbelow returned home later that afternoon, carrying with him an old umbrella. He leaned it against the table and said in a very matter-of-fact tone, "That's all the ticket was for, I'm afraid".

Julia was baffled and wondered what on earth could have happened to her mink coat. Not wishing to arouse suspicion, she tried to spark up a conversation by asking her husband where he had been in town that day.

"Oh I just decided to call on someone, that's all," he replied, nonchalantly, giving nothing away.

Julia had recently become suspicious of Howard also having an affair, and her doubts were magnified the very next evening when he uncharacteristically dressed himself up very smartly and splashed on some aftershave. As he prepared to leave the house, he gave a swift but vague explanation that he was visiting a colleague from work. Julia's suspicions grew and so, determined to catch her husband out, she decided to follow him. She rushed out after him, but lost sight of him by the tram stop further down the road. With her mind in a distressed whirl, she started walking the streets, deep in thought. What seemed like hours later, she sighed resignedly and finally turned to catch the tram home. As she glanced up the street, she just caught sight of Howard coming out of the Adelphi Hotel. As Julia had suspected, he was with another woman. To her utter surprise, that woman was wearing her beautiful mink coat. As Julia stood a fair distance away in stunned disbelief, Howard and the mysterious woman hailed a taxi, jumped inside and drove off.

Later that night, when they were both back at home, Julia was tormented by the state of her dysfunctional marriage. Unable to contain herself any longer, she accused her husband of having an affair. Howard angrily denied it but, before he could explain the scene outside the Adelphi, Julia confessed that she too was seeing someone else and that she wanted a separation. During her unplanned outburst, Julia announced that the mink coat had been bought for her by Adam. Howard Rumbelow could not believe what he was hearing. In a fit of fury, he threw his adulterous wife out of the house and bolted the door, vowing never to see her again.

Two days later, having calmed down and taken time to assess the situation, Julia formulated a plan of action. She caught the train to London and headed straight for her lover's house. As far as she was concerned, she was now a single woman and she was keen to be with Adam without feeling guilty. But it was not Adam who answered the door. There, standing before Julia, was the very woman with whom her husband had come out of the Adelphi just two nights back. Julia was speechless with astonishment.

It turned out that the mysterious woman was Adam Jones' wife. She explained to the emotional Julia that she had only just returned from a fortnight's holiday in Liverpool. Julia learned that her name was Lesley Jones, née Rumbelow, and that she was in actual fact the youngest sister of Howard Rumbelow; she was Julia's sister-in-law!

Julia groaned as the realisation dawned that Howard had merely been out with his sister and did not have another woman after all. He must have decided to give her the mink coat when he discovered it in the left luggage locker, probably because he felt his sister was more deserving of it than she was. To then discover that this new found sister-in-law was also the wife of her lover in London took some getting used to and she had to admit that she was the guilty party.

When Howard Rumbelow heard about the amazing coincidence he too was astounded. The revelations introduced a new, more honest element into the marriage and, after a lot of time and a lot of talking, there was eventually a reconciliation between himself and Julia.

Coffin Cries

In April 1922, a 50-year-old Liverpool man named William Banks woke up to find himself in complete pitch blackness. He squinted to try and focus on the strangely heavy darkness that seemed to be bearing down on him. With a yawn, presuming he was in his bedroom, Mr Banks tried to stretch out and turn over. His attempt failed as he scuffled awkwardly, unable to move at all. He felt hemmed in and as he tried to lever himself up by his elbows to get out of bed, he realised, to his horror, that he was not in bed at all. Just inches above his head he felt smooth, padded satin. The same material was brushing against his skin to the right and left. The unbelievable realisation that he was trapped in a coffin made his blood freeze.

"Oh God! They've made a mistake!" he stammered over and over in a breathless panic.

In an attempt to rationalise the unfathomable scenario, he tried to calm himself down. He struggled to lift the lid, but his efforts were futile and he felt a rising panic when he thought about the lack of air space. In utter desperation, he shouted out for help at the top of his voice and then stopped and listened, but everything was silent and his voice was engulfed by the muffled darkness. It was as silent as the grave, he thought cynically. Praying that he had not yet been buried, he tried again to push off the lid of the coffin, but it refused budge. Again he fell into a breathless panic as he started to think about being trapped underground. He envisaged the five feet of packed-down earth bearing down upon the coffin lid and screamed out again, feeling dizzy with anxiety.

Convincing himself that he had to save oxygen, William Banks wondered how on earth he had ended up in the claustrophobic coffin. He struggled to remember the events that had led to the premature burial. He recalled drinking at a pub off Edge Lane. There he had met a very pretty young woman named Blythe, who had said she worked as a secretary in North John Street. He and Blythe had drunk far too much, and she and another man had hailed a taxi cab to take him home, but he could not remember anything after that.

Time seemed to drag on. Banks was not sure if it was hours elapsing or minutes, but it felt like an eternity. He kept praying that it was all a nightmare and fervently repeated his Hail Marys. All of a sudden he heard a faint squeaking sound somewhere. It sounded like a rat. Imagination got the better of him in the stifling isolation of the coffin, and he listened to the loud scurrying noise and thought about the big red-eyed rats that were said to tunnel their way through graveyards; maybe they could smell him and were gnawing their way through the coffin. He imagined their bristly snouts nuzzling him and their sharp yellow teeth tearing into his flesh.

These distressing thoughts precipitated a severe panic attack. Then things got even worse. He felt something furry crawl over his neck: sharp, scratchy claws pricking his skin and long, twitching whiskers, tickling his Adam's apple. He hadn't been imagining the rat! A long, slithery tail whisked backwards and forwards over his throat, making the poor man almost faint with fear and revulsion. A hungry, graveyard rat was already in the coffin! He felt it scrabbling over his chest and sniffing at his left hand. Banks yelled out in terror, his heart pounding in his ears.

As his screams seemed to be swallowed up by the thick, satin lining, the sound of muffled footsteps and voices penetrated his airless prison.

"I'm not dead! I'm not dead!" William Banks screamed out.

The coffin was shaken, and he again heard voices mumbling outside. The footsteps then retreated, and Banks screamed for the people to come back. They did return minutes later and he heard them attempting to prise off the coffin lid. Banks also pushed as hard as he could against the lid.

"Thank God," he yelled, over and over again.

Moments later, the lid was finally lifted off and a bright light shone down at the ashen-faced William Banks. He shot up and gasped for air. Two policemen and a workman stood over him in the cellar.

It transpired that someone had just sent a boy into Lawrence Road police station with a letter. The letter explained that a man had been left inside a coffin in a cellar in an empty house in Edge Lane as part of an April fool prank. It was later surmised that the secretary William Banks had been drinking with had drugged him and that her boyfriend had imprisoned Banks in the coffin as an elaborate joke. Blythe was traced, her real name was Alice Kent and she was actually the stepdaughter of a minister from the Congregational Church in Marmaduke Street. When questioned, she and her boyfriend denied any involvement in the prank and nothing was ever proven. Where the jokers had got the coffin from was a mystery. On inspection, it was clear that they had drilled a hole in the end to ventilate it, and the rat, obviously left in the coffin to cause maximum fear, had in actual fact been tame. Poor William Banks had terrible nightmares about premature burial for the rest of his life. When he died years later, he was cremated according to his wishes.

Predictions

Strange Premonitions

It is claimed that the late and much-missed John Lennon experienced premonitions that he would be assassinated. He once stated that his fear of murder was one of the causes of The Beatles' break up:

"We were not bored," he once said, "and certainly did not run out of songs. I was paranoid about somebody trying to bump us off."

Apparently, Lennon told close friends that he felt as if he was being stalked by the Angel of Death. Furthermore, when his former road manager was shot dead by the Los Angeles Police, Lennon was heard saying over and over again, "I'm next, I know it!"

Others also had a grim foreboding of the ex-Beatle's violent end. During an interview taped on August 23, 1980, the late psychic, Alex Tanous, made a prediction. Tanous was asked by the show's host, Lee Spiegel, if something would occur in the next few months that would be of interest to rock music fans. In reply, Tanous stated:

"The prediction that I will make is that a very famous rock star will have an untimely death and this can happen from this moment on. I say untimely because there is something strange about his death, but it will affect the consciousness of many people because of his fame."

That interview was re-played in 1980 on 5 September, as part of NBC's *Unexplained Phenomena Show*. Just as had been predicted, on 8 December 1980, John Lennon was gunned down by Mark David Chapman in front of his home in New York City. Since Tanous had not specifically named anyone at the time, Speigel had drawn up a list of six possibilities, at the top of which had been John Lennon's name.

***

Nearer to home there have been other strange premonitions. I myself had one of these intriguing glimpses of the future in 1979. I was a child at the time, living in a house just off Myrtle Street. Over the space of two nights I had a strange recurring dream that I could see a vast gathering of helmeted men with shields. They were camped on a strip of green open space off Melville Place, on the border of Edge Hill and Toxteth. These figures were similar to Roman soldiers, except for the fact that their shields were made of a transparent material, as were the visors of their dark helmets. These Roman soldiers were also smoking, because I could see brief glowing spots of orange light as they anxiously puffed on their cigarettes. In the dream, I watched from the window of a darkened room. Each time, that was the moment that the dream would end, just as I would turn sideways to my mother, whose face was barely visible by the light of a lampost in the street.

In 1980, that dream was startlingly re-enacted when the Toxteth riots flared and reached the streets of my old neighbourhood. One night, a legion of police officers charged with riot sticks at the mobs down Grove Street and drove them back towards Toxteth. The helmeted policemen, with their transparent perspex shields (and some dustbin lids) then camped on the grassy area off Melville Place. My mother told me to get away from the window and turned off the light. We both looked out at the gathering. The police were smoking because I could see the incandescent tips of their cigarettes. It was at that moment that I realised that I had dreamt this scene the year before, and I turned to face my mother, whose silhouette was illuminated by the lampost outside. It was then that the faint tingle of déjà vu subsided. Why had I been given a preview of this future event? To this day I still don't know.

Another civil disturbance was mysteriously previewed in the 1940s by two Liverpool women. Maria Jones and Violet Keenan, both aged 32, were walking up the High Street in Wavertree in July 1949. They were busy making their way to a friend's house, when a bizarre sight greeted them. The time was around 8.30pm and before them a large gang of rowdy men, dressed in outlandish clothes was advancing down the road from the direction of the Picton Clock. These eccentric-looking men seemed like troublemakers. They were shouting and hitting out at other young men who were dressed in the more mundane suits which Maria and Violet were accustomed to seeing. The intrigued women whispered to each other as they stared at the unusual group.

The attackers wore distinctive clothes that the two women had never seen before. At closer quarters, Maria and Violet could see that the quaint costumes they wore seemed outdated, giving the impression that a cadre of Edwardian dandies had gatecrashed the 20th century to battle with the youth of the 1940s! One of these anachronistic brawlers wore a midnight-blue, calf-length overcoat, with black, tight-fitting trousers and the oddest pair of thick-soled shoes the intrigued women had ever seen. His hair was long and sleeked with oil and his quiff was swept upwards and forwards into a point. This quaintly-dressed youth was whacking a young man with a thick belt of some sort. A similarly dressed man brandished a long bladed knife that resembled a dagger, and he was heading towards the frightened, yet mesmerised, girls.

The cars travelling up the High Street halted as the colourful gang poured onto the road. Maria and Violet fled down a side street and took refuge in the nearby house of Maria's aunt. When they mentioned the funny-looking gang of mayhem-makers, people in the area returned blank looks. No one else had reported such a disturbance. Maria and Violet scanned the *Liverpool Echo* each day, but there was no reference to the commotion on the High Street to be seen on any page.

The strange incident was soon forgotten, that was until four years later, when Maria and Violet were again walking up the High Street in Wavertree, this time accompanied by their husbands. There, they witnessed an occurrence of what was to become a social phenomenon. A gang of so-called 'Teddy Boys' went on the rampage in the area. The gang of youths, dressed in the style of an Edwardian male, comprised of three groups that hailed from Wavertree, Old Swan and Huyton and had rendezvoused near Picton Clock before terrorising the people of the area. They charged down the High Street, armed with studded belts, knives, daggers and coshes, attacking any member of their age group who did not dress like themselves. The contemporary males, or 'mods' as the Teddy Boys called them, were looked upon as bores who deserved a good thrashing for conforming to the mainstream. Most of the girls on the High Street screamed as the resplendent marauders invaded the neighbourhood. However, it was Maria and Violet who were most dumbfounded, because they recognised the exact scene before them, they recognised the Teddy Boys as the strange-looking figures they had somehow foreseen in the phantom riot of 1949.

The Man Who Wanted to Know

If the very date and hour of your death could be determined, would you want to know? This choice was once offered to a wealthy tea merchant named John O'Shea. His story was related by his wife and sister in 1906.

In February 1906, a 56-year-old Wallasey man named John O'Shea owned a tea warehouse in Little Howard Street in North Liverpool. Business was lagging and he was resigned to expecting bankruptcy any day.

Mr O'Shea happened to be walking along Dale Street one afternoon on his way to see an old business friend, Edward Ellis, about a loan. This friend had achieved considerable monetary success since O'Shea had last seen him, five years earlier. O'Shea was obviously intrigued by his old friend's turn of fortune and asked him how he had managed to practically treble his personal wealth in so short a time. Edward Ellis dodged the question at first, but when the two men later went into a pub, the whiskey started to loosen his tongue.

The story he recounted was very bizarre indeed. He said that he knew of a Hungarian fortune teller named Mrs Zadora who had a genuine talent for seeing into the future. This woman had made many startling predictions which had come to pass. O'Shea was more intrigued than doubtful, for Ellis had said that Zadora had revealed the stock exchange prices a week in advance. Apparently, nine times out of ten her predictions were correct.

After some persuasion, Ellis later took John O'Shea to Mrs Zadora's small terraced house in Langrove Street in Everton. In a dingy back room, the fortune teller gazed into a crystal ball. The woman was aged about sixty and her eyes looked jet black.

"What can you see in Mr O'Shea's future?" Ellis immediately asked the dark woman.

After staring into the crystal globe for a long while, Mrs Zadora mournfully shook her head.

"The woman with whom he is having an affair, will die having his baby!" John O'Shea became visibly nervous. He was indeed having an affair with his sister-in-law and she was carrying his child. He turned increasingly pale as the fortune teller continued. "Mr O'Shea, there is something very bad here. Something very bad in your future."

Ellis had heard enough and decided that it was time to call an end to the proceedings.

"No, don't!" he cried.

The woman frowned but slowly covered the crystal ball with a velvet cloth.

"What did you see?" O'Shea urged eagerly, annoyed by his friend's well-intentioned intervention.

Ellis pleaded with the woman not to reply, but O'Shea insisted that she should reveal what she had seen. What she said had chilled him to the bone. Her strange eyes seemed to bore straight through him as she stared hard into his eyes and pronounced:

"You were lying in a hospital bed. You were blind and paralysed. Your wife and sister were there at the bedside. Your wife was crying and saying something about an accident. The doctors told her you'd be dead within months. I saw the date." She paused before continuing. "It was March the twenty-ninth."

O'Shea was terrified by the premonition and accused the fortune teller of being a charlatan. He argued aggressively with Edward Ellis and in a hurried panic stormed out the house.

A fortnight later, the grim predictions chillingly fell into place. O'Shea's sister-in-law died tragically in childbirth. The healthy baby survived, but the loss of the mother was just as the fortune teller had said. To the distraught O'Shea this indicated that the foreign woman had indeed been able to see into the future. Contemplating his doomed fate, he became immensely depressed; one evening he ended up feeling deeply morose, with a bottle of gin in one hand and a pistol in the other. He calmly placed the barrel of the pistol just under his chin. After a deep, heavy breath he fired one solitary shot.

Miraculously, O'Shea did not die immediately. The bullet smashed through his tongue, his upper pallet and emerged from the back of his head, leaving an horrific gaping hole in his skull. The wound was operated on, but O'Shea was left totally blind and paralysed by the injury. He died one week later, on 29 March, as his wife and sister sobbed at his side. The harrowing prediction had been completely correct. The details of this sinister story were confirmed by both Edward Ellis and O'Shea's sister and his wife.

The Bully and the Fly

In Edwardian times, a curious Irishman named John Hannigan appeared on the Liverpool scene. Nothing about the middle-aged man's past was known, except that he moved over from County Meath in Ireland in around 1905. The rest of his background was, and still remains, a blank. He did not seem to work, but was also never short of money, which was mostly spent in the public houses of Liverpool. He wore a pair of wire-framed spectacles and sported a trimmed moustache, and was said to have been handsome, with many a female admirer! Apparently, he was popular with most people because of his enchanting talent for storytelling and he was also known to be something of a psychic and philosopher.

On one occasion, in June 1908, he warned startled drinkers in the Vines pub on Lime Street that a great terror from the stars, that was capable of destroying England, was about to collide with the Earth. Some shuddered, knowing just how many of Hannigan's previous predictions had been strangely accurate, but most of the drinkers laughed, dismissing the Irishman as a drunken fool. However on the following day, *The Times* newspaper reported that an object, thought to be a gigantic meteorite, or chunk of a comet, had impacted into Siberia. The immense object from space had exploded with the fury of a modern thirty-megaton nuclear bomb. It had wiped out entire forests and incinerated herds of reindeer, and the enormously powerful shockwave had circled the Earth twice. Had the object arrived on Earth slightly later, England would have been instantly devastated, meaning that Hannigan's assertion had been curiously accurate.

During the 'stay-behinds' at the Vines, Hannigan would inevitably end up encircled by spellbound listeners, keen to hear his latest predictions, his supernatural tales of Ireland and his philosophising on the way society was progressing. On one such night at the pub, Hannigan's gentle accent lulled a captivated audience as he related his tales in front of a crackling coal fire. In the middle of his story, a well-known lout named Bob Stoneley staggered up to him and threw half a glass of stout into the Irishman's face.

"You didn't see that coming, John," sneered the drunken Stoneley mockingly. "Aren't you supposed to foresee things?"

Stoneley and two of his fawning cronies laughed as Hannigan quietly wiped his face and spectacles dry with a handkerchief. The landlord glared at Stoneley, but chose not to tell him to leave because of his violent reputation. Gerald McGuinness, a muscular seaman, confronted Stoneley, but the landlord quickly asserted that there was to be no fighting in his pub.

"I'll catch up with you later, Stoneley," McGuinness threatened under his breath.

"And I'll tear you apart," Stoneley retorted, as he started to rant about his younger days in the violent 'High Rip' gang and of how he was afraid of nobody.

Unruffled, Hannigan suddenly remarked, "Nothing frightens Mr Stoneley then?"

"Nothing," barked Stoneley.

"Not even death?" Hannigan's melodious voice rose, as a hushed silence spread over the room. "A piece of churchyard fits everybody, even you, Mr Stoneley," he added slowly.

Stoneley remained mute, visibly gripped by a mounting sense of dread.

"The hour of your death is near. Something in here will lay you in the ground," Hannigan warned the bully.

"Who? Who will lay me in the ground? Ged McGuinness?"

Stoneley's face turned red with smouldering rage.

"No, no, a fly will kill you," Hannigan stated languidly and without further elaboration.

There were twelve witnesses to his bizarre prediction. Stoneley left the Vines filled with nervous apprehension because he was well aware of the accuracy of Hannigan's predictions. How could a fly possibly kill him? He considered the diseases a fly carried; typhoid, cholera, and polio to name but a few. Feeling even more unsettled, Stoneley bought a stack of fly papers, just to be on the safe side. He also scrubbed his hands religiously before he ate, again, just in case! But his precautions were all in vain.

In July 1910, he was once again taunting John Hannigan in the pub. While maliciously laughing out loud at Hannigan's expense, a small fly flew directly into his mouth and lodged in his throat. Within seconds, Bob Stoneley choked to death as his cronies looked on in sheer horror ...

The Curse of Tich Maguire

In Liverpool in the early nineteenth century, there were many well-known local characters, but most of the interesting and colourful ones were from what you would call the rough end of society.

Prostitutes Maggie Mae, Mary Ellen and Tich Maguire are classic examples of famous, or rather infamous, Liverpool characters. Maggie Mae was a renowned streetwalker who used to wander along Paradise Street looking for gullible sailors. She was a gifted pickpocket and used to steal from her various clients in the waterfront pubs. Her good friend, Tich Maguire, lived just a few doors from her in Peter Street off Liverpool's Whitechapel area. Tich got her nickname because she was only five feet tall, although she was a beautiful woman of gypsy descent with long black hair and smouldering brown eyes.

In 1814, Tich went to a Dock Road tavern with a sailor named Barney Crow. He plied the harlot with gin, before taking her to an old warehouse in Sefton Street to have his wicked way. After the seedy act, he refused to pay up and proceeded to taunt the angry woman. The man's villainy surfaced further as he found a length of rope in the dilapidated warehouse. Laughing at Tich's attempts to challenge him, Crow wound the rope around his fist and smirked at Tich, who weakened with fear. She prepared herself for the fact that the violent sailor was going to choke her with the rope. Being a sailor, Crow was skilful at making all kinds of knots and he tightly bound the wrists and ankles of Tich Maguire, before then tying his scarf around her head to effectively gag her. He leant in close to sarcastically plant a kiss on the crown of her head, before leaving abruptly, wrenching the swollen wooden door shut behind him.

Tich Maguire was abandoned in the claustrophobic, all-enveloping darkness of the old warehouse, which was overrun with huge rats. Despite her tough reputation, she was terrified of the dark and also had a deep-seated phobia of rodents. She became panic stricken as she energetically struggled to try and escape. The night watchman heard her persistent screams and when he went to rescue her, he found her in an atrocious state. Some of the rats had nibbled through her boots and one had actually bitten into her hand. She sobbed uncontrollably from the sheer relief of being rescued in time.

A week later, Tich Maguire and Maggie Mae walked into a pub near Canning Place and there was Barney Crow, brazenly propping up the bar. The brute was trying his utmost to persuade an under-aged girl to accompany him outside. Tich could not hide her fury. Storming over to him, she sneered as she poured Crow's ale over his head and told everyone how the despicable sailor had left her tied up to rot in the rat-infested warehouse. Crow was visibly furious. The angry woman's tone deepened as she proceeded to warn him of her Romany descent. Grinning wickedly, with all the regulars in the pub looking on in animated suspense, she cursed Barney Crow and told him of her gypsy blood.

"I curse you, Barney Crow," she coldly announced, before launching into an embittered verbal assault on him. "You'll be drowned before long, with all the ship's rats."

Everyone present heard Tich Maguire's words of warning, but no one thought to take them too seriously.

Just one week later, Barney Crow was on board a ship that was bound for Jamaica, when it ran into a tremendous gale. The ship capsized and Barney Crow failed to make it to the lifeboat. What followed was truly gruesome. Crow scrambled onto a floating trunk from the sinking ship, where he probably thought he was relatively safe. However, a piece of splintered timber covered with about thirty rats from the ship floated directly towards him. The squealing rats jumped onto Barney Crow, despite his attempts to wrestle them off. In seconds he was covered with a mass of wriggling tails and twitching snouts. The claws of the terrified rats dug into Barney Crow as they clung onto him for their lives. The survivors in the storm-tossed lifeboat listened in dread to Barney, who could be heard shrieking and wailing, even above the howling gale. His ultimate fate is unknown, because the lifeboat was swept away in another direction, leaving Crow, and his uninvited passengers, tossing up and down on the waves in their precarious craft. Yet when the news of Barney Crow's nightmare final scenario reached the ears of Tich Maguire, she laughed out loud and danced on the bar of the tavern!

Near Death
and
Out-of-Body Experiences

Man Out of Time

In 2001, researchers at a Southampton hospital compiled evidence, after studying scores of patients brought back from the brink of death, which seemed to prove that people have glimpses of an afterlife when they are clinically dead.

The findings contradicted previous theories that so-called near-death experiences (NDEs) were the result of a lack of oxygen, because those reporting such experiences usually had the best reserves of oxygen. Researchers controversially concluded that the mind somehow managed to continue to operate after the brain had ceased to function during clinical death. The study found that one in ten heart attack patients had an NDE, comprising of emotions, visions and lucid thoughts, all experienced after they had ceased breathing and had no pulse.

Nearer to home, I once interviewed a man who had a fascinating NDE during an operation at the Royal Liverpool Teaching Hospital in the early 1980s. Mr Barrett, a 59-year-old Allerton man, was on the operating theatre table as surgeons removed polyps from his intestines, when he suddenly woke up. This phenomenon is known as 'awareness' and is the biggest fear of surgeons. The patient wakes, that is, becomes conscious, whilst still under the anaesthetic, but remains paralysed due to the pre med drug and so is unable to move, or even open an eyelid. Although still immobilised, the patient is able to feel the pain of every incision and in most circumstances can even hear the surgeon's conversations. Luckily, awareness is very rare.

On this occasion, Mr Barrett woke up and suddenly had the sensation of soaring upwards, through the ceiling of the operating theatre and up through the floors of the building. He was soon high above the hospital, floating at a great height. Mr Barrett certainly knew he was not dreaming. He had read about such out-of-body encounters and was overwhelmed when he realised that he was having such an experience. Then he noticed another strange thing. When he looked down at the streets of the city centre, there were many buildings he could not identify. In nearby Daulby Street, he saw a huge store where wasteland was supposed to be, and further along he noticed a glistening mirrored-glass building. In hindsight, this particularly striking building very much resembled the Roy Castle Lung Cancer

Centre, which had not even been built at that time.

The silent cars traversing the roads looked different and more streamlined than the normal cars with which Mr Barrett was familiar. It soon struck him that what he was seeing was not the present day Liverpool, but some future period. The disembodied patient floated across the city and saw huge futuristic buildings, including a sky scraper that towered over the Albert Dock.

Then Mr Barrett saw something which he later described as an awe-inspiring sight. Near to the waterfront site which is presently occupied by Cammel Laird, he could see enormous robotic cranes with mechanical hands busy at work. They seemed to be building a gigantic vessel which resembled what Mr Barrett could only describe as some sort of flying saucer! Catching his eye were tiny flashes of actinic light, as if arc-welders were at work on the titanic ship.

Before he could move in closer to determine just what was being constructed, Mr Barrett felt something pulling him backwards. This is a sensation often reported by people experiencing the latter stages of the NDE state. The Allerton man regained consciousness and found himself in the hospital. Straightaway he told his incredible tale about the journey into what had seemed to be the future. Most who listened to him thought that he had experienced nothing more than an hallucination from the anaesthetic, but just imagine what the alternative could be …

The Ultimate Answer

This is a bizarre story about guilt, curiosity and deadly knowledge. There is a certain series of streets near Goodison Park which infer specific words. The streets: Oxton, Wilmslow, Eton, Neston, Andrew, Nimrod, Dane, Wilburn, Ismay, Lind, Lowell, Index, Arnot, Makin, and so on in line, spell out, very distinctly, the words 'Owen and Williams'. In actual fact, Owen and Williams was the name of the firm of builders who built those very streets. A major shareholder in this firm was a Lancashire millionaire named Henry Williams.

Williams had become a millionaire after his father had died and left him his fortune. He felt immense guilt over his sudden wealth, which rumour has it may have been brought on after he heard a sermon by a

Welsh Presbyterian minister in 1886. Around this time, Mr Williams' behaviour became very erratic. He became completely fixated with the concept of death and started spending most of his time in and around hospitals. Specifically, he started to visit the Southern Hospital in Liverpool on a regular basis. In one instance he went over to a dying girl and sat with her, holding the sick little girl's hand as she passed away. Mr Williams softly stroked her frail hand, as if in a daze, he repeatedly urged, "What can you see?" The staff became concerned by the distracted man's persistent questions and eventually an alert nurse beckoned the doctor on the ward to literally throw Mr Williams out of the hospital grounds.

As the weeks went on, Williams's obsession with dying and what lies beyond the present life intensified. He talked at length with priests, vicars and ministers of every denomination and found that none of them could answer his question: what was it like after death?

It was not until he visited an equally eccentric man, a Dr McCheyne, and discussed the nature of death and the next world with him, that Mr Williams saw a potential solution to his inquiry. Dr McCheyne suggested something that today would have had him struck off the medical register. The eccentric doctor stated that he was confident that he had the means to stop Henry Williams' heart for a set period of time. He went on to claim that he could then revive him. He explained that he believed that this borderline between life and death, when the heart ceased beating and the brain became starved of oxygen, was the moment when many patients who were later resuscitated had reported intriguing glimpses of the 'next world'.

Amazingly, Williams became excited beyond belief at the prospect of his curiosity being satisfied once and for all, and hurriedly agreed to the highly unethical and dangerous experiment. Attended by a nurse, Dr McCheyne used ether and a solution of cocaine to bring Williams' heart to a halt. That part of the experiment ran smoothly, it was the restarting of his heart that became problematic. As Williams turned bluer by the minute, Dr McCheyne massaged his heart in utter desperation. There was still no response and Dr McCheyne became distraught as the clock ticked away. If left much longer, the brain would suffer irreversible damage and death would inevitably occur.

The nurse became increasingly anxious. She was all too aware of just how illegal an operation they were involved in, and shuddered at the fact that Dr McCheyne could well be imprisoned for such an unethical experiment and that she too could be tried for aiding and abetting him. After six seemingly endless minutes of electrified suspense and foreboding, the nurse detected a faint pulse in Henry Williams' wrist. His heart started to beat again, feebly at first, but gradually getting stronger. As he regained consciousness, the millionaire's body went into spasm, and he then proceeded to vomit, violently and uncontrollably.

Some thirty minutes later, Williams was calmer and was able to relate a very strange tale indeed. He described how he had travelled along a tunnel towards a bright and startling light, which is an overused description we hear regularly nowadays from people who have had a near-death encounter. Williams went on to explain how he had then found himself walking up large stone steps that were flanked on each side by huge pillars. At the top of this staircase there had stood a being, an amorphous snow-white column of immense power which gave off a terrific roar that sounded like a gigantic waterfall. He stated that it was God, claiming that he could not explain how he knew this, just that he had sensed it with an indisputable certainty.

Williams proceeded to give details about the figures he had seen coming down the stairs; they were faceless people draped in long, flowing gowns. These presences were in a limbo of some sort, but again Williams could not explain how he knew this. He claimed that at the top of the steep staircase, he communicated with God, which he described as feeling as if he was a vortex of life-giving energy. Williams went on to describe how he had told the force that he had come to Him for knowledge.

It was at this stage of his account that Williams became anxious. He stuttered as he explained how God had duly given him an overwhelming reply, which he described as the answer to everything - the meaning of life - contained in a single sentence of just seven words. The nurse and doctor waited and watched, enthralled by what they were hearing.

Apparently, the next thing that Williams had known was that he was alive again and recovering in the doctor's private room. As he sat up, he stared back at his dumbstruck companions with his eyes wide. He became visibly agitated as he struggled to remember what the all-important knowledge he had received from the other side had been.

Just moments later, with a look of sheer horror on his face, he slowly recalled what the momentous message had been, and animatedly recited the compact sentence to the nurse and doctor.

Events then took a very sinister turn. Within just one week, the nurse had allegedly committed suicide and the doctor was certified as insane. Williams is said to have told his secret to only six other people, each of whom supposedly also died within the year. Only one man who heard those seven mind-boggling words is said to have survived, a psychical research scientist, Sir Oliver Lodge.

Williams was also committed to a lunatic asylum and died from an epileptic fit eighteen months later. When the strangely linked deaths became public knowledge, religious mania was blamed. A persistent rumour circulated at the time, that the seven words of the so-called, 'ultimate answer' were written on seven separate pages and placed in a secret place. Be careful you don't ever stumble across them!

Bird's Eye View

In July 1969, a Kirkby grandmother named Elsie Keaton was put on a course of antibiotics to combat a severe attack of bronchitis. The pills had an adverse effect on the old woman and she started to get the shivers. Mrs Keaton was wheelchair-bound but very independent, so when her daughter, Joan, said she would stay off work to look after her, the elderly lady insisted that she would be fine on her own. She reassured her daughter that her neighbour, Mrs Jones, often called in for a cup of tea and a chat, so she was not completely alone, and Elsie's two granddaughters always called in on their way home from school at around four o'clock to check up on her.

At last, Joan reluctantly agreed to leave her mother on her own, out of a desire to respect her independence, but she demanded that she must call her at work if she needed her for anything whatsoever. Joan finally left, and Mrs Keaton relaxed and began reading a book, before shortly dozing off. In the following few moments, Mrs Keaton had what is known as an out-of-body experience. She later described the sensation as feeling as if she was literally floating up out of her body. As she drifted higher, she could see her house from a bird's eye view. During the sensational experience, she suddenly noticed a strange figure climbing over her neighbour's fence and entering her back garden. This figure was of a young man, who had a shaved head. She watched him sneak up to the house and try to prise open the kitchen window with a screwdriver.

Mrs Keaton was startled as she snapped out of her sleepy state; feeling fretful and uneasy, she wheeled herself over to the telephone and dialled the police straight away. She explained to the operator that she was certain that a burglar was trying to break into her home. The police arrived just in time, catching the youth who was still trying to force the window into Mrs Keaton's house.

It turned out that the would-be housebreaker was a dangerous escaped prisoner, who had been serving time in Walton Gaol for murder. His arrest and capture had been a lucky escape for the defenceless old lady.

Mrs Keaton could not explain the out-of-body experience which saved her life, but she remained convinced that her adverse reaction to the antibiotics had somehow been partly responsible.

Out-of-Body Revelation

One sunny winter afternoon in 1971, a 45-year-old Kirkby man named Glynn Roberts was driving his car through the Allerton area of Liverpool, when he suddenly had to swerve to avoid a cyclist. He lost control of the car and smashed into a lampost near the junction of Springwood Avenue and Woolton Road, about a hundred yards from Allerton Cemetery.

The car that Mr Roberts had crashed was, in fact, cobbled together from the halves of two different vehicles which had been illegally welded together. This abominable vehicle had crumpled on impact, dangerously trapping Glynn Roberts in the wreckage. Dazed by the violent episode, he looked around muttering to himself, "Thank God I'm okay".

As he weakly tried to shift himself across into the adjacent seat, he noticed something very remarkable. Somehow, there, sitting beside him in the car wreckage, was a man with blood pouring from his head. Roberts did not understand how the stranger, who looked exactly like a mirror image of himself, could have got there. In disbelief, Roberts looked down at himself to check if he had sustained any injuries, and discovered, to his complete surprise and horror, that there was absolutely nothing there. He had no body.

At that point, Glynn Roberts took on board the shocking reality; he was dead and the badly injured man in the driver's seat was himself. Roberts saw a young woman run over and gaze at the wreckage. An old man also approached, but did not acknowledge him. On the verge of hysteria, he wrestled himself free from the wreckage and began shouting at the bystanders, but they evidently could neither see nor hear him.

Soon, more and more people arrived at the crash scene and one teenaged girl even walked straight through Roberts, who by now was feeling nauseated by the awful scenario. He became extremely fearful. It felt like a living nightmare. All of a sudden, a woman walked directly over to him. He was quite surprised that she actually acknowledged his presence.

"You'll be okay, you'll be okay," she said, reassuringly.

The woman looked just like the Hilda Ogden character out of the old episodes of *Coronation Street*. She wore a hairnet with curlers underneath and a long, dark blue overall with a pinafore. She tilted her head, beckoning Mr Roberts to follow her across the road. She then passed straight through the railings into Allerton Cemetery.

"It's quieter here," she whispered.

She pointed to what was obviously a recently-dug grave, with no headstone.

"I'm supposed to be buried in there," she confided, in a mournful voice.

Glynn Roberts, despite feeling some pity for the ghostly woman, suddenly became overwhelmed with sorrow as he remembered his wife and also his five-year-old son, David, and baby daughter, Amy.

"I'm going back to my family," he announced insistently.

The woman then paused, as if in sympathy.

"You'll be back with the living soon, love." With a brightening expression, she told him that when he passed back over, she needed him to go to a specific house on Lorenzo Drive. "When you call there, tell Sophie that I left her something in the ventilator … Sophie's my daughter," she added with a sigh.

Suddenly, Glynn Roberts felt something physically dragging him backwards towards the crash scene. As he floated backwards, he passed by a grotesque-looking figure which made a grab at him.

"Get away from me," he shrieked.

The next thing Roberts was aware of was seeing two masked faces gazing down at him with startled eyes; the surgeon and the anaesthetist were lowering the oxygen mask over his face. Roberts fully regained consciousness later that day. His wounds had been terrible: the crash had caused him to suffer a broken nose, shattered collarbone and a comminuted fracture of the pelvis. As soon as he recovered, he wrote down exactly what the woman in the cemetery had told him.

After some months had passed, Roberts went to the address at Lorenzo Drive and, to his utter surprise, a woman called Sophie did actually live there. Understandably, she thought Mr Roberts' story was very far-fetched, but later telephoned him to say that her husband had just found an envelope containing £750 hidden in the disused central heating ventilator. Out of appreciation, Roberts was invited over to the house and he was shown a photograph of Sophie's mother. It was, without question, the woman that he had chatted to during his out-of-body experience. The photograph showed her standing in a garden, wearing a hairnet with rollers underneath. He learned that she had died of cancer, just days before Roberts had crashed his car near the cemetery.

Unexplained Mysteries

Baffling Babies

This is a sad and strange tale which was reported many years ago. In 1949, a four-year-old boy from Birkenhead, known only as Tony, was taken to his doctor after he had lost his appetite. The doctor examined the boy and became concerned about the state of his eyes. After further tests, the GP arranged for the boy to be taken to the Northern General Hospital in Liverpool. This obviously worried the young boy's mother and she urged the doctor to tell her exactly what was wrong. The doctor confessed that he was not certain; he reassured her that specialists in the University would soon know. A team of doctors and paediatricians arrived in a special ward at the Northern Hospital and made a long and exhaustive examination of little Tony, who clung tightly to his favourite teddy bear throughout.

On examination, it became clear that the boy's skin was starting to wrinkle and also his hair was thinning and turning grey. In a short space of time, he developed a stoop and over a period of just three weeks, he turned into what looked like a diminutive old man with white hair. His mother was inconsolable as she was forced to watch him ageing practically before her eyes. The doctors were baffled and could offer no explanation for his deteriorating condition.

Sadly, the child passed away a week afterwards. Modern research and medical development allow us to identify that the child was suffering from an extremely rare disease known as progeria, which is still barely understood even today. It is known that there are two forms of the disease. One manifests itself in children aged four, who seldom survive to their teens; the other version of progeria starts in adolescence and follows the same rapid degeneration.

Cases of the terrible illness are dotted throughout history. In Chester in 1890, a baby was recorded as being born with a full set of teeth, and when the midwife slapped its backside, the baby reportedly cried, "Stop that please!" This amazing speech was heard by the mother, midwife and two nurses, but was never explained. As the baby matured, its intelligence was so extreme that it was reading the Bible by the age of three and had mastered the Greek language by the time it was nine; a genuine child prodigy!

There have been numerous other reports of exceptional babies speaking words when they are newborn. Most reports are explained away as simply the sounds that babies make when they have mucous in their throat, but there was a report that a baby actually spoke in Liverpool in 1960. At the Oxford Street maternity hospital, a doctor, a nurse and a priest named Father O'Brien, allegedly heard a new born baby say the specific words, "Why have I come back?" The doctor delivering the baby was naturally dumbfounded, and the astonished priest described how the baby's eyes had been wide open as it spoke, and had beheld him with an uncanny intelligence.

Influenced in utero

Stranger still, in 1942 during a German air raid on Liverpool, a heavily-pregnant woman named Edna Jenkins of Toxteth was sheltering in a gloomy cellar, as she had been unable to find an air-raid shelter anywhere nearby. As she huddled in closer to the damp wall, she was horrified as a rat fell right on top of her. The rodent had been disturbed by the rumble of nearby exploding bombs. Edna yelped when the filthy creature landed on her stomach and she reflexively lashed out at it with her handbag. Once the air-raid was over, she thought nothing more of the revolting experience.

However, when Edna gave birth to a beautiful girl months later, the infant had a strange birthmark on her back. To Edna's horror, it was shaped exactly like the silhouette of a rat.

That tale is just as bizarre as an incident which took place in Paris in 1945. A local woman was accused of being a Nazi collaborator. When word got out, she was hounded out by the local populace and captured. Her hair was viciously shaved off, before she was roughly paraded through the streets of the liberated capital. The only thing that stopped the enraged French civilians from pelting her with stones, was the fact that the traitorous woman was heavily pregnant. Some months on from the ordeal, the unfortunate woman gave birth. Beyond explanation, her baby boy had a distinctive, sinister birthmark on his forehead; it was a swastika ...

The Bunny Man of Sutton Weaver

This is a very peculiar but sorrowful tale. In the summer of 1931, a gang of about six or seven children from Frodsham went to play in the countryside around Sutton Weaver, in Cheshire. The youngest of this gang was six-year-old Lizzie Davies, whom the rest of the children had a habit of leaving to trail behind. On this hot sunny day, this is precisely what happened. Lizzie was dawdling behind, picking flowers to make a daisy chain for her old battered-looking doll, which she always carried about, when a shadow suddenly rose over her.

When the girl looked up, she became numb with terror. Dropping the doll in fear, she sped off after her playmates with her chubby little legs legs turning to jelly. In a timid voice, she explained to her two older brothers, and the rest of the gang, that a scary man, with a 'bunny rabbit's' head, had scared her.

The group of children fell about laughing at the ridiculous claim, causing little Lizzie to burst into tears. As she sobbed, she complained that she wanted to go home. Still ridiculing her, the children began walking back, passing the very spot where Lizzie had seen the so-called Bunny Man. They saw no one there, and unfortunately for Lizzie, her favourite doll, which she had dropped in panic, was nowhere to be seen either.

Days later, the same group of children was playing in Beckett's Wood, when they bumped into an old poacher. The elderly man surveyed the group of startled youngsters for a few moments, before issuing a stark warning:

"You don't want to be comin' round 'ere, children, Big Ears will skin you!"

He went on to tell them the rumours about a bogey man who had long ears like a hare and long goofy teeth. He described how his body was covered in thick grey hair, and he could run as fast as a hare as well. The children immediately remembered Lizzie's strange encounter of a few days earlier, and pushed the reluctant six-year-old forward and forced her to tell the poacher about the Bunny Man she had seen. The old poacher sighed knowingly when he heard her story. He whispered to her that he too had seen the same weird-looking man many times over the years. The old man's voice hardened as he warned them that the Bunny Man had been known to kill children.

Next, he whipped out a skinned rabbit from his knapsack and thrust its grotesque face at the terrified gang, who ran off screaming.

Local legend has it that the infamous Bunny Man has been spotted on various occasions, but most people dismiss the claims as mythical, bogeyman tales. However, at around August time of that same year, a family from Runcorn was picnicking at a picturesque spot near Beckett's Wood. The two children, a girl and a boy aged eleven and twelve, ran off excitedly to explore and climb some trees, as their parents relaxed in the sun nearby.

Just moments later, the parents became concerned by the sound of loud screams in the distance. The young boy then emerged from the undergrowth and dashed up to them. He breathlessly cried that a horrible-looking man had grabbed hold of his sister. The worried father ran into the wooded area and found his daughter in a dreadful state. As she sobbed, she tried to explain what had happened. Through her choking sniffles, she described how she had been trying to climb down a tree and had slipped and lost her footing. Her fall had been broken by a large branch from which she had been left dangling. The branch had been too high off the ground for her to be able to jump and she had started to call for help.

She had looked around frantically for her brother, but saw him running off, scared away by a man with a deformed face, who seemed to have appeared from nowhere. She had been terrified as the freakish figure had then shinned up the tree, obviously making his way up to her. But when he had reached her, all he had done was gently help her down. She described him as having long teeth and strange ears, which seemed to reach down past his shoulders. His face and neck were covered in grey hair, which sprouted through the tattered shirt he wore. The man had tried to speak to her, but she said that his words were funny-sounding; he had seemed to have some trouble communicating. The strange man had then run away when the confused girl had screamed for help.

The police never investigated the bizarre story, and no one ever got to the bottom of the mystery, but there was a similar tale that circulated later on that year.

Rumour had it that the so-called Bunny Man was actually a deformed man who had become a hermit because of his unfortunate features. It was said that narrow-minded locals accused him of all kinds of evil things, but that, in actual fact, he had a heart of gold behind his frightening appearance. In 1932 he was said to have been found dead from self-inflicted wounds in the old shack in which he lived, near a place called Mare Clough. Close to the body, a child's doll had been found. Perhaps it was Lizzie Davies' doll, and perhaps it had been the only company the lonely Bunny Man had ever had.

The Living Dead

The following strange story was documented in a book called *Premonitions*, published in the late 1970s.

Joe Conroy was allegedly something of a confidence trickster who was known all over the Dingle area. He had once tried to go straight for a while, urged on by his long-suffering girlfriend, Stella, but it was not long before he was up to his old tricks again. He had once had a job in a factory near the Stanlow Oil Refinery where, after making friends with some of the workforce, he one day broke down and announced to them that his wife had died. He went on to describe how he was beside himself with grief because she had had no life insurance and he did not want to bury her 'on the cheap'. His factory workmates were very sympathetic and had a whip-around which netted Conroy almost £250 to help with funeral expenses. Of course, he had no wife and brazenly used the money to treat Stella to a day out in Blackpool, with no expense spared, using with her the excuse that he had won the money on the horses.

In 1971 Conroy became a frequent drinker at a pub in Park Street, called the Mersey Beat, situated in the south-end of Liverpool. Conroy was a natural storyteller and was quite popular in the pub, where someone would always bend an ear to his far-fetched stories. That November, Stella discovered that she was pregnant. Concerned about their future, she urged her layabout boyfriend to get a job to support her and their future child. Joe turned up, a couple of days later, with £90 in cash, claiming that he had won it in a poker game. However, that same week, Joe's friend, Kershaw, called at his flat in a drunken state, after a night in the pub. He unwittingly revealed to Stella that Joe had actually asked him to tell the drinkers at the Mersey Beat that he had died. All the drinkers had been so upset by the news, that they had given Kershaw over £90 towards the funeral, as well as many floral tributes. Stella thought Kershaw was joking, but the man picked up a copy of the *Liverpool Echo* and leafed through it to the Births and Deaths page. In the middle of the page, staring boldly back at her in print, was a tribute to a Joe Conroy, who had apparently died suddenly and, 'was missed by his girl, Stella'. Stella was naturally furious at the disgraceful antics of her untrustworthy partner, but Joe was completely unabashed and, with the ill-gotten £90, bought an old Hillman Imp.

One Sunday he and Stella used the car to drive up to Allerton Cemetery to put flowers on his mother's grave, which is where events took a very sinister turn. When Stella and Joe walked up to Mary Conroy's grave, they froze with shock, because on the headstone a new inscription had been engraved. The inscription read: 'Also Joseph Francis Conroy, 1940 to 1971'. Joe was naturally confused and more than a little apprehensive. He was convinced that it was not just some kind of joke, it was far too elaborate and costly for that. The pair left the gravestone in mutual fear, unable to comprehend what they had just witnessed.

A week later, Joe was drinking in a local pub called The Gardeners, when he suddenly dropped down dead, apparently from natural causes, at the age of thirty-one. After the funeral, many of the mourners glanced at the inscription on the gravestone, quite unaware that it had predated his death. The mystery remains unsolved to this day.

The Cottage that Moved

In 1871, a poor Welsh blacksmith who worked on the farm of an English landowner at Llanfor in Wales, was left a few hundred acres of land in the will of an old widow named Ruth Jones. The blacksmith was Robert Hughes and he had looked after old Mrs Jones on the neighbouring plot of land for over fifteen years. Out of gratitude and affection, she had bequeathed her little cottage and all her land to him in her will.

Robert Hughes' employer, a Lancashire landowner named James Deacon, wanted the land for himself and he subsequently hired two men to burn down Mrs Jones's cottage one night. Hughes was thus unable to move into the deceased widow's cottage. Instead, he had to remain in the run-down cottage on James Deacon's land, where he was forced to continue paying rent to the evil crook.

Hughes decided to approach a farmer from a neighbouring plot of land to try and sell him the inherited land, but the farmer was petrified of the infamous James Deacon and hastily declined. Still Mr Hughes did not give up hope and trekked miles to visit another farmer, but there it was the same story; the farmer would not entertain the prospect of buying any land near the belligerent troublemaker, James Deacon.

Night began to fall as Robert Hughes walked back to Deacon's farm in dismay; the land which was to form the basis of his new-found prosperity, was blighted by his wicked employer - no one would touch it. In the eerie woodland twilight, the blacksmith squinted to see where he was going. Suddenly, he lost his footing and fell down a crevice. It was overgrown with huge ferns and there was a shallow patch of water at the bottom of the deep hole. Hughes realised that he had stumbled into an old, forgotten well. He recalled how he used to visit the well years ago as a young child with his father. Robert rubbed his eyes as he recalled other happy memories, resigned to his present uncomfortable circumstances. Then he recalled how his father had always insisted that a wish made on the well would one day come true. Feeling somewhat sentimental, Robert Hughes voiced a wish for his luck to improve. Smiling now, he hoisted himself out of the well and continued on his way home.

That night, something very unusual happened. Robert Hughes was asleep in bed inside his dilapidated house, when the walls began to shake vigorously. A rumbling sound caused the foundations of the house to tremor. Plates began smashing as they fell off the walls and clouds of soot billowed down the chimney. The entire house jolted and Hughes was violently thrown out of bed. The startled blacksmith cowered under his bed and waited for the tremor to subside. Although afraid, he presumed that the disturbance was an earthquake and would soon pass. In that part of Wales they were not unheard of, what with Llanfor being situated on the Bala Fault Line.

Suddenly, all the commotion stopped dead and Robert Hughes could hear nothing but the wind whistling at the window. He ran downstairs to assess the damage and received the greatest shock of his life. When he gazed out of the window, he could no longer see James Deacon's house, which had previously dominated the view from the window. There were just trees there instead. Hughes, baffled, went outside to find that his entire cottage had somehow moved some fifty feet, so that it now stood on the land which Ruth Jones had left him in her last will and testament.

Hughes checked his home at first light and discovered, to his relief, that it had only suffered minor structural damage. As for James Deacon's house, a large crack was clearly visible, which ran from above the front door, right up to the roof. Later that week, Deacon's entire house collapsed in total ruin. He spent time and money having the cottage rebuilt, but as he was a superstitious man, he decided never to bother Hughes again. As for the lucky blacksmith, he later married and went on to prosper as a farmer in his own right. Right up until his dying day, Robert Hughes believed that his wish had been granted at the old wishing well in the wood.

The Queensway Tunnel Hitch-Hiker

Between 8 November 2000 and 25 January 2001, I received numerous reports of a phantom hitch-hiker in the Queensway Tunnel, near Crosshall Street. The descriptions I was given of the ghost are all identical: the apparition is female, aged about twenty to twenty-five, with long, sandy-coloured hair. She was seen by a policeman in the tunnel on the evening of Tuesday 19 December 2000. He claimed that she was standing about five hundred yards inside the tunnel near the Birkenhead entrance, gazing straight at the traffic. Seconds later, he noticed that somehow she had completely vanished.

A month before, a commuter also reported seeing an identical girl, this time in the middle of the tunnel, attempting to thumb a lift at 6am in the morning. Stranger still, he and a friend saw the same girl, along exactly the same stretch of tunnel, when they were returning from work at 5.30pm that evening. At the time, the witness had uneasily joked that she was a rather unsuccessful hitch-hiker, as she had been there for such a long time. However, when he thought about it, he realised that there could be no rational explanation for the fact that she had apparently remained in the tunnel for a full eleven and a half hours!

I also saw the ghostly hitch-hiker when I was on my way to work at six o'clock one morning. I was exhausted that evening after working overtime, so a friend drove me home. I could not believe my eyes when we drove back through the tunnel and I spotted the same girl whom I had seen earlier that morning. Unbelievably, she was there, in front of our eyes, one second, then gone the next.

"Did you see that!" my friend exploded, completely baffled by the apparition.

He was bemused because he had instinctively braked to avoid hitting her, but had then accelerated again when she had vanished into thin air. I remained quiet, relieved that he too had witnessed her disappearing act. If I had been the only one in the car, I would have thought that I was going completely nuts!

The spookiest encounter took place that same month when a motorcyclist named Liam actually stopped in the tunnel to pick up the hitch-hiker. The girl had said she was going to Huyton. Accepting the lift, she had then taken the spare helmet off the motorcycle rack and placed it firmly on her head, before climbing onto the pillion seat. Liam and the girl had then ridden off, but when the motorcyclist emerged from the tunnel, he realised that she had vanished from the pillion seat and the helmet was back in its place on the motorbike's rack. There seemed to be absolutely no rational explanation.

Does anybody else out there know about the ghostly hitch-hiker of the Queensway Tunnel? If anyone does, I would love to hear from them. A number of people report that she has been seen on various occasions since as far back as the mid-1960s, but I wonder who she was?

Invisible Barriers

The following strange incident was reported to me in November 2000. A couple returned to their house off Birchdale Road in Warrington, after a night out with friends. The couple, Brian and Alyson, went straight to bed as soon as they got in. At about three o'clock in the morning, Brian got up to go to the toilet. On his return, he went to pull the bedroom door shut behind him but found that he could not close it properly. Presuming that the carpet was blocking the door, he wrenched it open and sleepily walked towards the landing to switch on the light, not wishing to wake his wife up by putting on the bedroom light.

As Brian trudged out of his bedroom, he encountered some kind of obstruction which he could not actually see. The sensation felt like a sharp electric shock, which stunned him and flung him backwards into the bedroom. Brian's nose ached from the bump and he looked at his bare arms, which were covered in prominent goosepimples and the hairs were all sticking up on end. He sat on the bedroom floor for a few moments in dazed disbelief. He pulled himself to his feet and walked back to the landing. He reached out with his hand and tried again to move forward a few paces. In the now lit passage of the landing, he once again felt the strange obstruction. It felt like a wall of cold granite and when he pushed his hand into it, he again felt an electric shock sparking up his arm.

Alyson was roused by her husband's muffled yelps and through a yawn she asked him what was wrong. As she squinted to focus on him, she noticed how concerned he looked. Brian described the enigmatic presence on the landing to her, and insisted that she also come and feel it, just to prove to him that he was not losing his sanity. As she stood next to her husband, rubbing her eyes, Alyson too reached out and felt the invisible wall. Brian was fascinated, he rolled up a sock and threw it at the barrier; to the amazement of them both, the sock bounced right back at them.

At first light, Brian telephoned his friend across the road, a policeman named Phil. Understandably, Phil thought his friend was winding him up at first. He called at the house across the road with a colleague on their way to work. Brian appeared at the bedroom window and threw his front door key down to Phil, inviting him to come up to experience the weird obstruction blocking the passageway.

Phil and his cynical associate were astounded when they also encountered the strange barrier and found it completely impassable. Then, just as swiftly as it had appeared, it suddenly was no longer there.

Phil, a rational man, chose to believe that it had been a build up of high tension static electricity, generated from the new carpets that had just been fitted at the house. Despite various attempts, no one has been able to properly explain what the bizarre barrier was.

***

I have heard of many other similar accounts of invisible barriers in the north west region of England. I recall one incident that was alleged to have taken place in July 1995, in a multi-storey car park at the bottom of Mount Pleasant in Liverpool. A female student named Sarah was becoming more and more frustrated as she repeatedly tried to park her Ford Fiesta. The car seemed to keep bumping up against something as she reversed into the space, but there was no visible obstruction in her mirror view. Her boyfriend was with her and knew she was a good driver, so he got out and looked under the Fiesta to see if something just out of sight was obstructing the vehicle. Just as they had thought, there was absolutely nothing there. Once again, Sarah slowly reversed into the space; this time the vehicle loudly collided with something invisible, which caused an echoing clanging sound. After trying once more, Sarah backed into the seemingly empty parking space with no trouble whatsoever. She and her boyfriend were left perplexed.

Perhaps there is some mischievous force at large in that part of Liverpool, because there have been other similar incidents reported close to that multi-storey car park. One morning in the summer of 1983, a bemused constable from the Smithdown Lane Traffic Police Headquarters, noticed two lanes of cars waiting at a green light, at the bottom of Brownlow Hill, near the Adelphi Hotel. The policeman investigated and could not believe his eyes or ears. Right before him, eight cars had simultaneously stalled at the lights and their drivers were having great difficulty restarting their engines. Minutes later, the engine trouble ended abruptly and all the cars were able to move off amid the din of impatient motorists beeping their horns in the hold up. Had it been a cold morning, the weather could have been blamed for the mass stalling of the engines, but in this instance it was a sunny summer morning. Perhaps the incident was just coincidental. Many years ago when I was learning to drive, I stalled on Edge Lane and the person behind me slammed on the brakes, causing him to stall also. But how would eight cars, in two lanes of traffic, stall at exactly the same time? We'll probably never know.

Freaky Forces

Forces of unknown origin, affecting vehicles, even including carts and horse-drawn carriages, have quite a long history. In the Old Testament's *Book of Numbers,* Chapter 22, Verses 21-33, there is the account of Balaam and his ass, where God forbade him to go in a certain direction. Balaam tried to go in the forbidden direction but his ass shied away from that path. He then beat the poor animal to force it to obey his wishes, but the ass backed against a wall, crushing Balaam's leg. In the end, the ass lay down in the road and refused to budge, even though Balaam beat it. The explanation given in the Bible is that the animal's strange behaviour was caused by it being able to see an Angel of the Lord, which was obstructing its path.

In Fazakerley's Higher Lane, a strange entity has been encountered since 1950 which has caused accidents by pushing vehicles off the road and even causing their tyres to lift above the road's surface. Sometimes this presence on Higher Lane has been seen to materialise into a black amorphous shape, which often rises up from the road to assume the outline of a human figure.

In February 2001, a driver telephoned me at BBC Radio Merseyside to describe how a sudden powerful gust of wind had pushed his car off the road on Higher Lane near Sparrow Hall and almost caused a fatal crash. When the motorist had got out of his car, he noticed that the weather was perfectly calm and not even a leaf was moving on the trees. This odd account is just one of dozens which I have heard of, or read about, over the years.

Our present knowledge of physics is limited and does not serve to explain the unusual forces mentioned in this chapter. At present, there are just four types of force in the known universe. The most powerful of these is the powerful nuclear force which holds atomic nuclei together, but it is such a short-range force that it has no effect outside the nucleus. Then there is the electromagnetic force, which is 140 times weaker than the nuclear one. The electromagnetic force is evident in most electrical machines, radios and cell phones. There is also the 'weak nuclear force', which is one hundred billion times weaker than the electromagnetic one and is only evident in atomic reactions. The fourth, and highly mysterious force, is gravity, the weakest of all the forces. Most people imagine that gravity is a powerful force but in actual fact, gravity is so weak, that every time a child lifts a spoon to his mouth, he is overcoming the gravitational pull of the entire Earth. Could there be other forces, as yet undiscovered by science, which could explain poltergeist activity, telekinesis and some of the incidents described in this chapter?

Scientists consider that there are still unknown forces, but it may be some time before we can find explanations for them. Centuries ago, no one even suspected that radio waves, gamma rays or infra red and ultra-violet radiation existed, simply because no one had invented the hardware to detect these radiations. We are in a similar predicament today, although the force fields of science fiction have been recreated on a limited and largely impractical scale. All computer ink-jet printers today use a static charge to guide and propel ink through a nozzle without even touching the fluid.

On a similar note, in the 1970s, the United States Army carried out an experiment using electrostatic fields to generate a force field. A machine similar to a Van der Graaf generator, powered up a high tension field of static electricity which successfully deflected a speeding bullet. The impetus behind the experiment was that perhaps the infantryman of the future could be rendered virtually bullet-proof by carrying a nuclear-powered force field generator which could deflect projectiles fired at him.

Perhaps when we are able to create our own force fields and invisible barriers, we shall be nearer to finding out who, or what, is behind the sinister intrusions I have just mentioned.

The Black Cloud

During the 1974 power cuts, when the country was often plunged into darkness, a group of children and a number of adults in the Huyton and Dovecot areas of Liverpool reported a very strange phenomenon: a billowing black cloud that chased after them at ground level.

The first reports of this cloud-like phenomenon came from the children's playing fields at Longview Lane. A Mr O'Brien was taking his two corgis for a walk one evening when there was an unexplained powercut and all the streetlamps went out. The only light remaining glimmered weakly from a thin crescent moon. Suddenly, Mr O'Brien's dogs started barking madly and when he turned around, he was confronted by a jet black cloud, about fifteen feet across and ten feet high, rolling straight towards him. The dogs were still barking frantically, but he could not actually see them. As the strange cloud closed in on him, he decided to run for his life. A few minutes later he was forced to slow down by a stitch in his side and he looked back and saw that the cloud had vanished. Unfortunately, so too had one of the corgis. That dog was never seen again.

Mr O'Brien was distraught and told his sister about the frightening encounter. She insisted that he had been seeing things, but her friend, a Mrs Parle, remarked that her children had told her about a similar-sounding cloudy mass which had also chased them near Whiston Lane. The children claimed that a police panda car had driven slowly past the strange cloud and that the police had actually witnessed the cloud too.

About a fortnight later, during another powercut, a man in Dovecot was on his way to a mobile shop to buy candles, when he suddenly felt icy cold. He sensed something to his left and when he turned, there was what he could only describe as, 'a huge black thing' before him. According to him, it looked like a cloud, but he felt it was alive in some sense, from the way it flew in the direction in which he was about to run. When the man sped home, he felt sick with fear and refused to go out of doors until the next morning.

The most frightening account came from a thirteen-year-old boy named Tony, who encountered the ominous cloud during daylight hours. Tony was wearing a pair of novelty shoes, with a compass in the sole, that his mother had just bought for him. He took off one shoe and looked at the compass that was incorporated in the heel, to see if it really did point north. Suddenly, the compass needle went berserk, vibrating violently, just as something blocked out the sun. A jet-black cloud suddenly emerged out of nowhere and drifted about in front of him. He became flustered as something seemed to be choking him. He felt as if he was being starved of oxygen and in his distress he dropped the shoe and staggered home, coughing and spluttering, desperately trying to regain his breath. His mother returned to the spot to retrieve the missing shoe and she described how the surrounding air had felt somehow electrically-charged.

As soon as the powercuts stopped, the menacing cloud was seen no more. It was alleged that several people had vanished around that time in Dovecot. Specifically, one man named Brian Henderson went missing; his brother presumed he had gone to work in Manchester, but strangely he never ever got back in touch again ...

The Quarry Demon Terror

This spine-chilling tale is taken from a very old, out-of-print book called *Bygone Wavertree*. The township of Wavertree once had a large quarry, known as a delph, located near Woolton Road and Lance Lane. In March 1837 the local governing body, The Select Vestry, decided to put railings around the old quarry because it was becoming too deep and dangerous.

Around this time, a local man named Fowler was digging in the quarry to obtain stones for his garden wall, when he came across some broken pieces of a black stone jar. Intrigued by the strangely attractive pieces, he gathered them up and made his way home, weary from all the digging he had done. His new garden wall was never completed. The man was later found dead. No cause of death was ever established.

The room he was found in offered no evidence of a struggle or an attack. Everything seemed tidy, and even the man's slippers were placed at the foot of his bed, ready for him to slip on the next morning. When he was discovered, he was lying on his bed, pale and gaunt, just as if he was soundly sleeping. However, there were numerous fragments of the unusual vase scattered about the room. On later examination, the pieces were thought to date from a Neolithic settlement in Wavertree thousands of years back in the stone age.

Not long after that inexplicable occurrence, something terrifying was seen in the spooky old quarry. A teacher was walking past the quarry as she guided five of her young pupils to Sunday school. As they crossed over the road, she glanced back to check that all the children were still with her, when she saw what could only be described as a thick dark mist rising in billows out of the quarry. She was completely stunned as she noticed that the heavy mist appeared to somehow possess a pair of smouldering red eyes. In petrified astonishment, she huddled the children together tightly and yelled for them to run with her as quickly as they could. The animated mist clung closely to the tracks of the screaming group, relentlessly pursuing the teacher and her little brood down the street until they breathlessly fled into the sanctuary of a nearby church. Only at the church door did the murky-looking apparition cease its pursuit.

That very night, the same teacher was heard by neighbours screaming in extreme agony from her bed. It seemed that she had been abruptly woken from her slumber by a sudden sharp pain. She had cried out uncontrollably as something lacerated first her legs, before then spreading onto her arms, chest and face, causing excruciating pain. In the middle of this harrowing experience, she also exhibited stigmata on her head, causing her forehead to bleed heavily. The blood left a sinister stain close to her hairline, as if she had been forced to wear a crown of thorns. She could not explain the unbearable events of that night, nor the haunting mist that had harassed her little flock.

Even scarier, exactly one week later, two men were taking a short cut through the deserted quarry. As they picked their way awkwardly over the rocky gravel, they noticed that some random rocks were being pelted at them. Presuming that it was just some mischievous kids, they turned around to see where they were. To their complete disbelief, the vast and open quarry was utterly deserted, and yet the stones kept raining down on them. Bewildered, the men looked at each other quizzically, whilst trying to dodge the shower of rocks. All they could surmise was that something invisible was hurling stones at them, there was no other explanation. The attack increased in intensity, so much so that the men were now being badly injured. In fear and confusion, they both ran for their lives, without daring to look back.

The suspicious goings on did not cease there. At a farm near Olive Mount, two cows literally dropped dead one evening without showing any signs of illness and no explanation for their deaths could be determined. That very same night, the intimidating dark mist, with glowing eyes, was seen again, this time by two girls. The unfathomable thing had surfaced slowly in front of their eyes before moving menacingly towards them. As they backed away from it, the mist seemed to follow them. The frightened girls turned on their heels and ran into an old mill, at the place where Mill Lane is now situated, in an attempt to escape the dark, imposing presence. Afterwards, it came to light that one of the poor girls had been pregnant at the time and she suffered a miscarriage as a result of the traumatic experience.

As is so often the case with supernatural incidents, the reports of the awful apparition went unheeded, that was, until a local priest witnessed the misty entity coming towards him down a lane near Woolton Road. The priest had been alerted to its presence when he had heard a dog barking fiercely at something down the lane. When he went to investigate, the dog let out a single, final, high-pitched yelp, before collapsing and becoming enveloped in the malevolent mist. The animal slumped to the ground and then began to convulse, before proceeding to foam at the mouth.

The stunned priest could only watch in impotent horror as the dog suffered horribly for some moments before its muscles finally seized up altogether, and the poor thing froze into a grotesque pose. It was dead! This distressing experience was the ultimate test of faith for the priest, who spun quickly round and ran for his life. On confiding his strange story to a colleague, he learned to his dismay, that an old priest from Childwall had recently reported having had a similar encounter. He too had met with the suspicious presence from the quarry and had suddenly died from heart failure shortly afterwards.

The insidious 'thing' in the quarry became the subject of much local gossip. Children were forbidden to play near the place and nobody took the once-popular short cut through the quarry anymore. Rumours proliferated even more when, on the following Sunday, a certain George Hynes went missing. His family could not explain his disappearance which was totally out of character for him, and grew increasingly concerned as each evening passed and he did not return home. Their worst suspicions were confirmed when his shattered corpse was found amongst the boulders at the bottom of one of the steep quarry faces; his neck had been violently broken from the presumed fall.

The mystery was unravelled, as a result of the police investigation, which revealed that, on the previous night, George Hynes had boasted to friends at his local pub that he was afraid of nothing. He had proceeded to bet money on the fact that he could visit the eerie quarry, completely alone, at midnight, without a worry; it was to be the last thing he ever did.

Terrifying encounters with the demonic wraith continued to occur with sickening regularity. At a cottage on Dunbabin Farm, a six-year-old boy let out a scream when he noticed pair of glowing eyes staring through the window of his bedroom. He had been so spooked by what he had seen that he had hastily packed a knapsack and run away from home to stay with his uncle in Dudlow Lane. The terrified young lad had refused to re-enter his room, absolutely insistent that the sinister eyes proved that his room was haunted.

Reports of the mist spread even further afield. Two elderly sisters resided at a house on Lance Lane. They died within minutes of each other after the maids and a servant had fled from the place in sheer terror. When interviewed about the circumstances, the staff nervously claimed that something indescribable had swirled down the chimney and chased a frightened kitchen maid. The elderly sisters may have died from shock, as they both had weak hearts. However, the so-called, 'ghost scare' was blamed for contributing to their sudden deaths.

In response to the much-dreaded encounters with the cursed mist at large in Wavertree, eight local priests and ministers pooled their resources to combat its evil influence. They were keen to cleanse the village, as well as trying simultaneously to allay increasing public disquiet.

An elderly priest from the Holy Trinity church claimed, with insistence, that the local quarry was in fact the lair of a demon. He instructed the local authorities that the only way to end the turmoil looming over the town was to turn the Wavertree windmill around so that its shadow would cast a huge cross over the quarry at sunset. Believe it or not, the priest's advice was taken and the plan was carried out. When the sun dipped below the horizon at the end of the day, the enormous, cross-shaped shadow of the windmill stretched over the gloomy quarry.

Almost at once, a deep, low, rumbling sound from deep within the quarry was heard by everyone in the district and crowds of fascinated locals rushed to the scene to witness the dramatic and sudden collapse of the mysterious place. Perhaps it was a mere coincidence that the massive landslide occurred when it did, but those in the community who had lived in fear of the evil mist needed no convincing.

After the dramatic events of that night, Wavertree Quarry was silenced at last.

Mysterious Mister Bill

The following story concerns one of the strangest and creepiest incidents I have ever investigated and I have been involved in some spine-chilling cases. As I write my account of the following tale I am on my own and, although I consider myself to be a seasoned, almost shock-proof ghost investigator, I feel distinctly uneasy and during this paragraph I have already glanced over my shoulder twice.

Before I relate the eerie story of Mister Bill, a word of warning. After you have read this tale, either move on quickly to another story, or watch a soap, or listen to a CD. Surf the net, or visit a friend, but whatever you do, do not lie in bed tonight dwelling on what Mister Bill is, and if possible, do not even mention him again.

First, here's a case which may throw some light on the true nature of the uncanny Mister Bill. Many years ago, in 1972, an American psychiatrist named Wilson Van Dusen was working at Mendocino State Hospital in California. He treated a number of patients who said they were being stalked by phantom people. Van Dusen specifically sought permission to interview these supposedly schizophrenic individuals to fathom out the nature of the psychoses which were causing them to experience such persecution complexes. As his examinations progressed, he was not prepared for what he uncovered.

Firstly, a young female patient visited the doctor and claimed that she had a phantom lover. By asking a series of probing questions, Van Dusen tried elicit to exactly what she meant. She sighed deeply and nervously explained in a timid voice how it had all been a joke at first. Apparently all of her friends had been dating someone apart from her so, out of sheer wounded pride, she had invented Stephen, "just for heck of it", she said. Her tone hardened and her expression changed as she went on to say that now she could not get rid of him. She shook uncontrollably as she confided in the doctor, explaining that she had told him repeatedly it was over, but that he would not take no for an answer.

Van Dusen calmly asked her where exactly Stephen was. He inquired politely whether he was nearby in someplace, or whether he was just in her mind.

"He's standing next to you right now," she stated curtly.

"Would I be able to have a little chat with, with um, Stephen?" Van

Dusen asked carefully.

"Sure," the girl replied, flashing her eyes up at the person only she could see.

Van Dusen proceeded to ask Stephen what he was, and why he would not break up with his patient; the girl relayed everything that her unseen and unheard companion told her. She had never read a psychology book in her life, yet she elaborated in amazing detail as she forwarded Stephen's replies to the psychiatrist's questions.

Van Dusen began to feel very uneasy as he gradually received a strong impression of a presence in the room. He definitely felt as if someone was standing just to his left. At one point in the interview the girl made an unexpected announcement.

"Stephen has just told me that you were reading a book on Greek myths yesterday."

Van Dusen immediately visualised the copy of the Greek text sitting far away in his house on his bedside table, where he had placed it the night before. He was shaken to the marrow, there was no way his patient could have possibly known that. He was still digesting the implications of all this when she came out with the following statement:

"Stephen says he started off as an hallucination in my mind, but he was able to evolve a consciousness of his own."

Van Dusen was a man of science and reason and could not accept the concept of possession, but he felt that the girl he was interviewing *was* somehow possessed by an exterior intelligence. In the end, the psychiatrist reached a dead end in his investigations and was sadly unable to help the troubled girl. In an endeavour to understand her psychological state, he subsequently interviewed a series of apparently schizophrenic patients, and discovered that many of them were well-balanced and far from mentally dysfunctional. It seemed as if they too were actually being shadowed by independent entities of some sort. Again, on interviewing these patients, it transpired that these invisible stalkers exhibited a remarkably wide range of knowledge that encompassed psychiatry, literature, astronomy, religion and musical composition.

Van Dusen was so fascinated by the experiences of his patients, that he wrote about the phantom individuals in his book, *The Natural Depth of Man*, in 1972. The book truly is a fascinating read in terms of psychological exploration and theory. The strangest fact that comes to light in Van Dusen's investigation is that many of the menacing entities share distinctive names that are reported by patients living in many different areas of the world. One of these names is 'Mister Bill'.

Out of all of these inexplicable 'hallucinations', Mister Bill has one distinctive attribute: he has allegedly been seen by people other than the person who is supposedly hallucinating him. Even more frightening is the fact that he has been seen in the United States, Europe and even right here in Liverpool as well. His appearance is very sinister indeed. He is always seen wearing a black, tight-fitting garment, not unlike a body stocking, with a black balaclava-like headpiece which gives the bizarre apparition a somewhat medieval look. The face of Mister Bill is said to bear an uncanny resemblance to the old glove puppet, Punch, with a prominent and ruddy-coloured nose; his eyes have black borders and are often described as being evil-looking, whereas his voice sounds contrived, like the projected sound of a ventriloquist.

Now, in the occult world there are intriguing things known as 'tulpas'. These are solid, tangible projections that are born of human imagination, but gradually manifest themselves on the physical plane. They are also known as 'thought forms'.

In the 1920s, a remarkably tough-minded and highly independent Frenchwoman named Alexandra David-Neel, undertook a long and hazardous journey into Tibet on a pilgrimage to seek out the fabled practitioners of the ancient art of magic. She was a wise traveller and knew a charlatan when she saw one. On her travels, Alexandra visited many strange and intriguing places and met various magicians, gurus and accomplished yogis, who demonstrated their perplexing powers. The Frenchwoman was very impressed with one particular magician who not only gave a demonstration of levitation, but also showed her how to construct a quasi-solid form that he had generated through sheer willpower. The Tibetan magician called the apparition he had created a tulpa, and seriously warned Alexandra how these 'children of the mind' often escaped out of the control of their maker to become independent beings, often becoming mischievous and even murderous.

The magician gave Alexandra the specific instructions which enabled her to create her own tulpa. Alexandra was completely intrigued and decided to create a harmless character: a short fat monk who looked innocent and jolly. For a period of several months, the westerner shut herself away to concentrate her thoughts and practise the rituals prescribed by the magician. In the end, and much to her amazement, she succeeded in creating the phantom mirthful monk, but found the astounding exercise in willpower mentally draining. The corpulent monk would follow Alexandra about, but in time he started performing various actions his creator had not commanded him to carry out.

What was even more disturbing was the fact that the tulpa was not a subjective hallucination; it was seen on many occasions by everyone else besides Alexandra. Gradually, over the weeks, the monk became more troublesome. He developed a sarcastic, mocking personality as a decidedly evil streak began to surface. In the end, Alexandra David-Neel spent six long, hard months trying to rid herself of the terrible monk.

Perhaps something similar happened when the ubiquitous Mister Bill turned up in the house of a family in Liverpool. This tulpa, if that is what it was, turned up on a photograph taken on the Christmas Eve of the year 2000. A 45-year-old man named Jimmy had taken a photograph of his family and friends in his living room. In January of the new year, when the developed snaps came back from Max Spielmann's, Jimmy smiled as he shuffled through the glossy prints because of the memories they triggered. His smile faded abruptly when he noticed on one print a strange figure in black standing in the hallway in the background, just visible through the doorway.

The looming figure was not noticeable on any of the other photographs. It looked like someone in a grotesque mask, depicting a weird, big-nosed character. The presence of the figure really unnerved Jimmy, and he showed the photograph to his wife, who thought it was extremely creepy. Both were unsettled by the intrusive presence in the picture and decided not to show it to their young son, just in case it frightened him.

Well, the photograph was later sent to me. I placed it on a computer scanner at high resolution and zoomed in on it. I agreed it was an eerie figure, but asked Jimmy and his wife whether they could be absolutely sure that someone in fancy dress had not been standing in their hallway when the picture was taken. They were positive that no one other than close family had been at the house that day. Furthermore, no one present had been remotely dressed like the peculiar man in black.

Then the mystery took on a new and terrifying dimension. The couple's eight-year-old son, Danny, started to wet his bed. He told his mother that he had started to wake up in his bed in the early hours of the morning, unable to move a muscle. Sometimes he complained of a 'horrible man in black', who appeared in the room during these frightening periods of paralysis. Danny was asked to draw the scary night visitor, and his parents immediately recognised that the drawing matched the likeness of the black clad weirdo in the Christmas photograph which, of course, Danny had not been shown.

A few weeks later at four o'clock in the morning, Danny ran screaming into his parent's bedroom. He cried out that the figure in black was in his room again, sitting on top of his wardrobe. Jimmy grabbed the baseball bat which he kept under his bed and was reserved for any late night intruders. He told his wife to dial 999 and then stormed towards his son's room. Jimmy stopped in his tracks for a moment as he heard very faint singing coming from inside Danny's bedroom. He kicked open the door and paced his way in, only to find that there was nobody there. The only indication of any disturbance was the heavy wardrobe, which had somehow toppled over onto the bed.

It took a week before the family finally calmed down. Danny was most unsettled, and when a doctor examined him he informed his concerned parents that he was a highly-strung child, who was possibly hyperactive. Wracking his brains for any cause for his distress, Jimmy wondered if the troubled child had heard them talking about the man in black captured on the Christmas photograph. Maybe he had, and maybe that had triggered a series of vivid nightmares.

Things seemed to settle down over the following weeks, until Valentine's Day, 14 February. Jimmy's wife was gift-wrapping a boxed set of CDs which she had bought for her husband, when she distinctly felt someone breathing down her neck. She turned round, fully expecting to confront someone, but there was nobody there. Feeling jittery and on edge, she went to check the kitchen door which led to the yard and found that it was fully locked. When she returned to the living room, she noticed that there was now childish writing on the blank gift tag which she had been about to write; it rested on the parcel containing the CDs. Vividly upon the tag, in blue ink, someone had scrawled the words, 'Mister Bill'. Naturally, she was bemused and more than a little unsettled.

When she mentioned the name to me, I wondered if it was a mere coincidence. Perhaps Danny had written that name on the parcel, maybe as some Freudian protest because he wanted his mother to give the gift to him, instead of his father. But the creepy events did not cease there.

The next day was a Thursday and that evening the window cleaner called to collect his payment from Jimmy. He also had a strange tale to tell. He said that on Monday afternoon, while the house was empty, he had been cleaning the living room windows and had seen something which made the hairs on the nape of his neck stand on end. A man in black, whom he thought looked like something from the Middle Ages, had been sitting on the sofa in the parlour. He was bolt upright and gazing straight ahead at the clock on the wall. The window cleaner described to them how he had banged on the window, expecting a response, but apparently the figure had remained stock still and did not even blink. The window cleaner had become suspicious and called his colleague from across the road to come and have a look at the stranger in black; he too saw the man and was equally intrigued. They called over Jimmy's neighbour, but when she looked into the parlour through the bay windows, she saw nothing, there was definitely no one in the room.

Understandably, Jimmy and his family have now left that cursed house in Liverpool and I remain curious about the mysterious Mister Bill.

A Stony Embrace

This is a particularly eerie mystery that allegedly took place in Liverpool during the severe winter of 1962. That year, fifteen-year-old Nancy Greenwell of Dovecot was introduced to Robert Jones by her cousin. Robert lived in Ince Avenue, and it became a regular occurrence for him to take Nancy round to his friend's house almost every night. As the couple started courting, Nancy became completely obsessed with Robert. She used to scribble his name on her exercise books at school, talk incessantly about him all day long and would spend all her pocket money on him, plying him with records and other gifts. Robert's father soon insisted that his son should get a job instead of wasting his time just lounging about with Nancy. Hostility built up between them and in the end he warned Robert never to bring the girl home again.

As an act of rebellion against his strict parents, Robert and Nancy started mixing with a local gang. They used to wander around Anfield Cemetery, amusing themselves in the dusky evenings. One evening, Nancy was on the bus to a friend's house, when she saw something that shattered her heart. As the bus was travelling up Queen's Drive, she happened to glance out of the window and, just as she did so, she saw Robert, in a bus shelter, locked in a passionate embrace with Nancy's best friend, Tina.

In a state of shock, Nancy remained firmly seated on the bus as the tears started to flow. When she reached her stop, she got off and wandered around in a complete daze. Robert's friend saw her walking into Anfield Cemetery looking very forlorn. The distressed girl was next seen by a school friend named Maureen Davies. Nancy was very emotional as she told Maureen what had just happened. In near hysterics, she exclaimed that she wanted to die, before running off between a row of gravestones.

It was getting late and was now extremely dark. Inside the tree-framed cemetery, away from the streetlamps, it was almost pitch black, and Maureen was too frightened to carry on looking for her friend. She left hastily, and made her way round to Nancy's parents, where she informed them that their daughter had seemed devastated by what she had seen and looked almost suicidal. They were obviously concerned, and became increasingly worried when Nancy had still not returned home by eleven o'clock that night. They alerted the police, who searched the deserted cemetery, but Nancy Greenwell was nowhere to be found. Then the beam of a policeman's torch flitted over something curious in the distance as he was on his way out of the vast necropolis. There before him, was a huge, white, marble statue of a man, about nine feet in height, with its arms stretched out before it. Draped across the arms of this imposing figure was the limp body of Nancy Greenwell.

That night, temperatures had plunged to five degrees below zero, d the post-mortem established that the girl had died from hypothermia; yet how she had ended up in the arms of the statue was never solved. Then came another mystery. The statue of the stone man had no inscription on it and, after investigation, it was discovered that it had never been part of any grave or memorial. There were no records of who had erected it, and consequently it was eventually removed by the Parks and Gardens Department.

It later came to light that people in the Anfield area regarded the unidentified statue as having a supernatural reputation, and some seriously alleged that the marble figure had actually been seen to move on several occasions. Its last resting place was a private garden in Tudor Court, on the campus of Liverpool University, facing the University Baths on Oxford Street.

One night in 1975, that nine foot marble statue vanished into thin air. Its present whereabouts, and its role in the death of Nancy Greenwell in 1962, remain a mystery to date.

Did Lincoln's Murderer Escape to Liverpool?

One August night in 1862, Abraham Lincoln was riding out to the Retired Soldiers' Home, situated in the woods of northwest Washington, when he heard a sudden gunshot. As a bullet whistled past his head, Old Abe, his faithful horse, stampeded at the loud report and raced pell-mell all the way to the Retired Soldiers' Home. When Ward Hill Lamon, Lincoln's self-appointed bodyguard, heard of the attempted shooting, he informed the President that the shot had probably been fired by some Southern extremist. However, Lincoln flatly disagreed; he denied that anyone had deliberately tried to shoot him and instead offered the suggestion that the almost fatal shot had probably come from the gun of a short-sighted hunter in the woods. No definite conclusion was arrived at, but security was tightened as a result of the incident.

In the spring of 1864, rumours circulated in the press of a rebel plot to assassinate the President, but Lincoln persistently dismissed all the conspiracy stories.

"Even if it is true," Lincoln told the newshounds, "I do not see what the rebels would gain. If they kill me, the next man in line will be just as bad for them."

Shortly after issuing this provocative statement, Lincoln received a steady stream of hate mail. The first malevolent missives frightened him, and the death threats which followed naturally made him even more apprehensive. But as the letters started to arrive ever more frequently, and in even greater numbers, the President became desensitised and he began routinely filing all the serious threats away in a big envelope marked 'Assassination'. Despite the intimidation, Lincoln refused to alter his lifestyle.

"I know I'm in danger," he confided to William Seward, the Union Secretary of State, "but I am not going to worry about it."

In the following year, Lincoln's heavy work schedule and chronic insomnia began to wear him down. On the rare occasions when he did manage to snatch some sleep, he hardly ever dreamed. But on the night of 9 April 1865, he experienced the first of a series of disturbing dreams. He described the first dream in vivid detail to his wife, Mary, and Ward Hill Lamon:

"I could not have been long in bed when I fell into a slumber, for I was weary. I soon began to dream. There seemed to be a death-like stillness about me. Then I heard the subdued sobs, as if a number of people were weeping. I thought I left my bed and wandered downstairs. There, the silence was broken by the same pitiful sobbing, but the mourners were invisible. I went from room to room; no living person was in sight, but the same mournful sounds of distress met me as I passed along. It was light in all the rooms; every object was familiar to me; but where were all the people who were grieving as if their hearts would break? I was puzzled and alarmed. What could be the meaning of all this?

Determined to find the cause of a state of things so mysterious and so shocking, I kept on until I arrived at the East Room, which I entered. There I met with a sickening surprise. Before me was a catafalque, upon which rested a corpse wrapped in funeral vestments. Around it were stationed soldiers who were acting as guards; and there was a throng of people, some gazing mournfully upon the corpse, whose face was covered, while others were weeping pitifully.

'Who is dead in the White House?' I demanded of one of the soldiers.

'The President,' was his answer, 'he was killed by an assassin!'

Then came a loud burst of grief from the crowd."

Lincoln, his intense description complete, looked to his wife, Mary, who was trembling at the eerie account.

"That is horrid. I wish you had not told it," she said, glaring sternly at him.

"Well, it is only a dream, Mary," Lincoln replied reassuringly. "Let us say no more about it, and try to forget it."

But Lincoln could not forget about it. Similar dreams of death continued to haunt what little sleep he had, until that fateful date of 14 April.

Upon that day, at precisely 3pm, John Wilkes Booth entered the Kirkwood House bar in Washington DC, and began drinking heavily. The 26-year-old actor was a handsome, olive-skinned man with raven coloured hair. He sported a heavy, walrus moustache which he had grown in an attempt to mature his youthful countenance. Booth had made his professional debut in 1855 at the Charles Street Theatre in Baltimore, where he had performed as Richmond, in *Richard III*; he had acquired quite a following of female admirers in the mid-western and southern theatrical circuits. His most recent stage appearance had been as Pescara, in *The Apostate*, at Ford's Theatre in Washington DC, on 18 March. Booth was a talented, but undisciplined actor, who was probably at his best playing melodramatic heroes and villains, but he had once impressed Abraham Lincoln with his performance in *The Marble Heart*, at Ford's Theatre on the night of 9 November, 1863, just a week before Lincoln spoke at Gettysburg. Booth was a headstrong man with a passionate interest in his country. In terms of political persuasion, he secretly sided with the Confederacy, despite the fact that his family were keen supporters of the Union.

That evening, several drinkers in the bar recognised Booth, and some noticed that the actor seemed to be visibly anxious. He was spotted an hour later at Derry's Saloon, where he ordered a medium-sized bottle of brandy. He finished the entire bottle, before moving on to Taltavuls Saloon, which stood next door to Ford's Theatre. In this dreary saloon, Booth and George Atzerodt, another Confederate sympathiser, confirmed the final arrangements for the assassination of Abraham Lincoln and the Vice-President, Andrew Johnson. The agreed plan was that Booth was to dispose of Lincoln, and Atzerodt would slay Johnson. Both assasinations were orchestrated for that evening.

Meanwhile, back at the White House, the Lincolns had made plans to visit the theatre that evening to see the well received production of *Our American Cousin*, by Tom Taylor. Mary Lincoln was complaining of a headache. She wearily explained to her husband that she was not too keen on going to the theatre, but Lincoln, unaware of the fate awaiting him, coaxed her into changing her mind.

Detective George Crook had been seriously concerned over the safety of the President ever since the suspicious initial attack. He tried to insist that Lincoln did not go to Ford's Theatre, adamant that the public appearance would be dangerous. But the President assured him that everything would be all right.

"Then can I stay on duty, sir, and accompany you to the theatre as an extra guard?" Crook asked with determination.

"No, you've had a long, hard day's work and must go home," Lincoln told his worried friend, patting him on the back. He slowly walked with Crook to the portico of the White House and told him to go straight home to get a good night's rest.

Now, because of last-minute visitors, Lincoln and his wife did not actually get away from the White House until 8.15pm, which was when the Presidential carriage finally rolled out into the fogbound street. Inside the secure coach, Lincoln was smartly attired in a black overcoat and white kid gloves; Mary looked stunning, dressed elegantly in a grey silk frock with a matching bonnet. Major Henry Rathbone and his fiancée, Miss Clara Harris, accompanied the Lincolns. The bodyguard for this specific theatre visit was John Parker; a somewhat strange choice, for he was reputedly a lazy oaf with an appalling record of drunkenness, insubordination and gross inefficiency. However, it was Parker who had been sent ahead of the Lincolns, and who was already at the theatre preparing for their arrival.

At 8.30pm, the Presidential carriage emerged from the swirling mist and pulled up in front of the theatre. Lincoln and his wife hurried from the carriage to the foyer, eager not to miss much more of the beginning of the play, which had already started. Rathbone and Miss Harris followed closely behind. Ford's was packed with the top brass of the Union army and assorted Washington socialites. Upon spotting the President in the state box, which overlooked the stage, the audience exploded into a standing ovation, and the orchestra began to play *Hail to the Chief.* Lincoln proudly watched his admirers until the music had died down and the last ripple of applause had faded away. He then sat himself down in the specially-made rocking chair and turned his attention to the actor, Harry Hawk, the male lead of the play, who ad-libbed:

"This reminds me of a story, as Mr Lincoln would say."

The enthusiastic audience roared with laughter, and Lincoln smiled, whilst leaning in to whisper something to Mary. Major Rathbone and Miss Harris were seated in the same box, and were affectionately holding hands.

As the play continued, bodyguard, John Parker, began to pace the hallway that led to the state box. Just ten minutes later, the negligent guard abandoned his post to visit the saloon next door, leaving Lincoln completely unprotected.

In Taltavul's Saloon, the irresponsible Parker stood less than six feet away from John Wilkes Booth and his fellow-conspirator, George Atzerodt, who were confirming their final plans over one last drink. In the same bar, Lincoln's valet, Charles Forbes, and Francis Burns, the coachman from the Presidential carriage, were also enjoying a swift drink. The conspirators parted. Atzerodt was now so intoxicated and frightened of the repercussions of the intended assassination plot, that he, unknown to Booth, had decided to abandon the plan.

As Lincoln watched the beginning of the third act of the play, he complained of feeling a strange chill, so Mary slipped her hand into his, and embraced him lovingly.

At 10.15pm, the door directly behind Lincoln flew open, and John Wilkes Booth entered the state box brandishing a Derringer. He pointed it directly at the back of the President's head, less than five inches away, and ruthlessly pulled the trigger. A resounding gunshot rang out. The bullet entered Lincoln's head just behind his left ear and swiftly tunnelled through his brain, becoming lodged behind his right eye. The President's right arm jerked up convulsively, and he slumped forward. Mary reached out instinctively and caught her husband while Wilkes just stood there, a menacing silhouette almost enveloped in gunsmoke.

Every face in the theatre turned to the state box. Some thought the gunshot had been a theatrical gimmick, especially when John Wilkes Booth emerged from the smoke wearing a ridiculously outsized black felt hat. But when the young intruder next produced a dagger and stabbed Major Rathbone, the audience realised that this was not play-acting at all.

"The South is avenged!" Booth shouted passionately, as he leaped from the state box, intending to land on the stage. However, as he plunged, he caught one of the spurs of his highboots in a regimental flag and crashed down onto the stage, breaking his left shinbone in the fall. The assassin left the theatre via the stage door, staggering on his wounded leg. At the back of Ford's, in considerable pain, Booth struggled onto his awaiting horse and rode off into the fog.

Major Rathbone was astounded by the violent outburst. He gripped his arm, which had been gashed to the bone by Booth, in an attempt to stem the heavy bleeding. He was in an extreme state of shock and seemed to have been rendered speechless. Mary Lincoln let out a terrible scream as she cradled her now seemingly lifeless husband, while Clara Harris hollered out over Mary's screams, "Stop that man! Stop that man! Won't somebody stop that man! The President is shot!"

But Booth had already fled from the scene of the crime.

"Is there a doctor in the house?" someone in the audience cried.

But there was no answer. Pandemonium broke out, and people were shoved to the ground in the aisles as the audience stampeded for the exits. The English actress, Laura Keene, who had been playing the female lead in the abandoned play, yelled out:

"For God's sake, have presence of mind and keep your places, and all will be well!"

But the commotion continued. Charles Leale, a young army doctor, fought through the panicking crowds until he reached the President's box, where Clara Harris was trying to console Mary, who was at this stage weeping hysterically. Leale lay the President on the floor and acted quickly. After detecting no pulse in Lincoln's wrists, he removed the blood clot from the wound to relieve the pressure on the brain. Noting that Lincoln's breathing was shallow, Leale efficiently jarred open his mouth and proceeded to apply artificial respiration. Soon, an elderly doctor also arrived in the box and instructed Leale to massage the President's left breast. As Leale did so, the other doctor raised and lowered Lincoln's arms. The resuscitation procedure had been successful, and the President's heart started beating irregularly. Slowly he started to breathe unaided, although he remained unconscious. The doctors carried him out into the misty night and across the street to Petersen House, where a War Department Clerk had a vacant room. Lincoln was gently laid down on the clerk's four poster bed, as Rathbone and Miss Harris carefully assisted Mary over, to be with her dying husband.

The news of the shooting spread like wildfire throughout Washington, and a procession of government officials headed for Petersen House. When Secretary of War, Edwin Stanton, heard the terrible news about Lincoln, he stated, "Now he belongs to the ages".

Stanton took over the government. He and a federal judge took down testimonies from a gaggle of witnesses, who confidently identified John Wilkes Booth as the President's assassin. Under Stanton's ruling, the city was put under martial law; he co-ordinated dragnets to find Booth, and a reward of $100,000 was offered for the capture of the attempted assassins. But Booth had something of a head start after his despicable deed, because the telegraph lines out of Washington DC went mysteriously quiet for several hours after Lincoln was shot, so the rest of America was not aware of the President's murder for a significant amount of time. This perplexing fact was not made public at the time, and has never been satisfactorily explained.

Abraham Lincoln, the sixteenth President of the United States, died, without regaining consciousness, at 7.22am on 15 April. His body was subsequently taken to lie in state in the East Room of the White House. It soon dawned on the widowed Mary Lincoln and Ward Hill Lamon that the President's unsettling dreams of death had now come to pass.

Eleven days after the untimely death, a man believed to be John Wilkes Booth was tracked down by a Union Army patrol. The time was 2am, and the army patrol had cornered the fugitive in a barn on the Richard Garrett property near Port Royal, Virginia. Although he was surrounded, without a chance of escape, the man refused to come out, and so the soldiers ignited the barn to smoke him from the premises. But the man inside the building never got a chance to flee from the flames, because Union soldier, Boston Corbett, poked his rifle barrel through a crack in the barn wall and blasted the villain in the back of his neck. The man was dragged outside, but he died soon afterwards from his fatal wounds.

However, on examination, the dead man did not even resemble John

Wilkes Booth. Booth's hair was black, but the dead man's hair was undeniably naturally red, and his stubby nose was quite unlike Booth's aquiline nose. When a physician who had once attended Booth set eyes on the corpse, he remarked that he could find, "No resemblance whatsoever. Never in a human being has a greater change taken place".

Despite the physician's important comments, the red-headed corpse was treated as the assassin and transported to Washington DC. There, the body was secretly interred under the flagstone floor of Washington Arsenal Prison. It was exhumed two years later and then stored in a pine box in a warehouse. The body was left untouched until 1869, when President Andrew Johnson had the box moved to a funeral home, where Booth's brother, Edwin, a famous actor, finally claimed it. Edwin arranged for the coffin to be reburied in an unmarked grave at Greenmount Cemetery, Baltimore on 26 June 1869. He was haunted by the memory of his brother's evil deed, and it is interesting to relate that in 1893, Ford's Theatre, the scene of John Wilkes Booth's atrocious crime, collapsed for no apparent reason during the funeral of Edwin Booth.

On 13 January 1903, some thirty-eight years after Lincoln's death, an old man lay dying in a lodging house in Baltimore. The 65-year-old asserted that his name was David E George and that he was an actor. No one in Baltimore had ever seen him tread the boards, so most people regarded him as a Walter Mitty type of character. But upon his deathbed, as he struggled to gasp for his final few breaths, he uttered a startling confession to his landlord and doctor.

"I killed one of the greatest men who ever lived."

"He's delirious," the doctor sighed dismissively.

"No I'm not," retorted the weakening Mr George. "I killed Abraham Lincoln."

The doctor shook his head with a defeated look. He could do no more for his patient.

"Do you doubt it?" whispered Mr George. "I am Booth."

The landlord was intrigued by the old man and humoured him.

"How did you escape then?" he urged.

Allegedly, Mr George went on to then explain that he had escaped to England after killing Lincoln, where he had travelled around London and Liverpool, staying with friends. This seemingly random explanation is, in actual fact, perfectly plausible. Liverpool had been the hometown of Booth's thespian father, Julius Brutus Booth, who had relations in Liverpool, and had even performed at Liverpool's old Theatre Royal in Williamson Square. John Wilkes Booth had also lived in Liverpool as a youth, so he was familiar with the city and its layout. Then a thriving port, Liverpool had benefited much from the slave trade and so was very anti-Lincoln during the American Civil War. At the time, Cammell Laird had even turned out several vessels for the South, including the famous *Alabama*.

Before the mysterious Mr George could elaborate further on his fantastic claim, he slipped into a coma, from which he never recovered, dying later on that day.

The landlord's curiosity had been aroused by the strange confession and so he convinced the doctor that there was a slim possibility that Mr George may have been Booth. The medical man unenthusiastically took out his notepad and wrote down all the identifying marks he could see on Mr George's body. These notes were later analysed by two doctors who had attended John Wilkes Booth. They revealed that the scar on Mr George's neck was in the same place where an unsightly, benign tumour had been removed from Booth's neck; the deep scar on Mr George's left shin tallied well with the site of the shin-bone injury which Booth would have received when he fell from the state box onto the stage at Ford's Theatre on the night of the assassination. However, one distinguishable injury did not tie in. The dead man had a scar on his right hand, but no one seemed to be able to recall a similar scar on Booth's right hand. That was until 1904, when Joseph Heidelsen, a man who had been a programme-seller at Ford's Theatre in his youth, came forward to fuel the controversy. According to Heidelsen, Booth had been rehearsing at Ford's Theatre one afternoon, when he had accidentally got his right hand caught in the curtain-raising mechanism and suffered a deep gash as a result. Thus the third scar was satisfactorily explained.

So, was David E George telling the truth? Was he really John Wilkes Booth? Or was he just an old dreamer with a fevered mind, trying to make a name for himself before he died? How can we discount the curious comments of the physician who had treated Booth when he examined the red-headed corpse? And the testimony of the programme-seller at Ford's Theatre who was well-acquainted with Booth? All the unanswered questions surrounding the fate of John

Wilkes Booth indicate that someone in power must have not only allowed the actor to escape after he had killed Lincoln, but also somehow arranged for the red-headed fall-guy in the barn to be treated as the accused and then murdered. If this was the case, it would suggest a sinister conspiracy as far-reaching as the intrigue that surrounded the assassination of John F Kennedy.

Hauntings

The Ghost of the Old Northern Hospital

The following strange and touching tale is said to have taken place at Liverpool's Old Northern Hospital in the late 1950s. Two men who were both seriously ill shared a room at the hospital and subsequently developed a close friendship. 59-year-old Jim Sullivan had suffered a stroke that had left him blind and partially paralysed. The other patient, seventy-year-old Wilfrid Edwards, suffered from pancreatic cancer.

Edwards began to notice that Sullivan, who was a bachelor, had scarcely any visitors. He felt extremely sorry for the lonely man, lying there blind and unable to move, so in a kindly attempt to console him, Edwards began to stand at the window and describe all the things he could see, just for Sullivan's sake. His considerate gesture became a regular event, and he spent a great deal of time evoking the view from the window to entertain his friend.

The poetic imagery which Edwards conjured up in the darkness of Sullivan's mind was vivid. He would paint eloquent verbal pictures of the beautiful park, where graceful ivory swans could be seen gliding upon its mirrored lake and of the various trees and spectrum of flowers that graced the picturesque landscape. So articulate was he that he was able to convey whole scenes to his stricken companion: translucent rainbows arching over the Mersey, burning amber sunsets, and ships coming and going on the river.

As Edwards described the great panoramic canvas of life going on outside the hospital, the bed-bound Sullivan regained some of the hope he had lost in the extremity of his illness. He started to feel as if life was worth living again and consciously determined to get better. With a new, positive perspective, Sullivan began to feel that he wanted to take part in the wonderful life which we all take for granted.

A few months passed before Jim Sullivan began to experience slight tingling sensations in his toes. When he concentrated, he could sometimes even wriggle them. Excitedly, Edwards alerted the nurses and soon a doctor was at Sullivan's bedside to investigate the miraculous claims. Over the course of just one week, Sullivan impressed his specialist by managing a full smile and even mustering the strength to gesture the thumbs up sign.

Not long afterwards, Sullivan's rapid recovery took another positive turn and he regained his sight unexpectedly one morning. Elated, he struggled awkwardly up onto his elbows. His newly-restored vision was slightly distorted and his eyes strained to focus as they hungrily searched the ward. Just across from his bed lay Wilfrid Edwards, the man who had inspired him to get better with his rousing descriptions of the wonderful world beyond the hospital window. Sadly, his friend and companion of many months had just exhaled his final breath and was lying, limp and lifeless, upon the bed. His still-open eyes were staring directly at the window.

Tearfully, Sullivan struggled to raise himself enough to just glimpse out of the window. He was curious to see for himself the stunning views which Edwards had described in such intricate detail. However, what he saw gave him the shock of his life, because the window actually looked out onto a high, brick wall. Sullivan felt a strange warmth overcome him as he realised that his companion had actually been making up all those stunning descriptions in order to give him hope; they had all been for his benefit.

Years on from that touching occurrence, claims have been made that a mysterious presence has been seen on that very ward, near to that very window. It was said that in 1960, another stroke victim insisted that he often saw a ghostly figure at one of the windows in that specific hospital room. The patient explained how the apparition, who was not a threatening presence, would appear in the early hours of the morning.

Furthermore, in 1965, a night nurse was halfway through her shift, when she became aware of a gentle voice nearby. She could not make out where the delicate voice was coming from, but as she listened carefully she could just discern the soft tones of a man. She was insistent that his voice sounded reassuring, as he vividly described, in great detail, a scene of children playing in a picturesque park. Several of the patients also claimed to have heard the disembodied voice that night. Although a number of patients had passed away in that room over the years, the nurses remain adamant that it is the ghost of Wilfrid Edwards, perhaps still trying to inspire the sick to get better.

Bridegroom Revisited

In the year 1870, a twenty-year-old man from Ormskirk named John Hargreaves was picnicking with his cousin in the Lake District, near Kendal. He was breathtaken as he admired the awe-inspiring pastoral scenery which spread before him. His attention was suddenly diverted when a beautiful girl, aged about sixteen or seventeen, caught his eye. Her name was Sarah Parr, the youngest daughter of a local farmer who had recently fallen on hard times. That evening, after Hargreaves' persistent pestering, the country girl was introduced to him by his cousin. John was so mesmerised by her beauty, that he decided to stay at his cousin's cottage for the remainder of the summer, just so that he could spend time with Sarah.

Very soon a loving relationship blossomed between the innocent pair. However, the sweet romance was dramatically catapulted back into reality at the end of July, when Sarah informed John Hargreaves that she was carrying his child. At first, the couple was elated, but John's father, a wealthy landowner, was furious when he heard the news. He issued his son with the ultimatum that if he married Sarah Parr, he would be excluded from his will and his monthly allowance would be stopped. It seemed that John Hargreaves senior had plans for his son to marry the daughter of a wealthy Liverpool shipwright instead.

John made a decision. He ignored his heart and chose monetary gain over the love of his sweetheart. That evening, he took Sarah for a walk to one of their favourite haunts, a rocky ledge above a fast-flowing stream which came straight off the fells. In this beautiful spot, he coldly announced to Sarah that he was returning to Ormskirk, and that he was doing so without her. Naturally, Sarah became hysterical.

As he was walking away from her without glimpsing back, she screamed pitifully for him to return. He steeled himself to ignore her, for he was nearly as distressed as she was, but walked on nevertheless, until he heard her shriek, "I will haunt you until your dying day!" At this dramatic claim, Hargreaves glanced around just in time to see the desperate girl leap from the rocky ledge into the boulder-strewn stream below. The brutal tumble broke her delicate neck, and it is said that the entire stream turned red with her blood.

Just one year later, Hargreaves was marrying the prestigious Mary

Holt in church, some accounts say it was St Oswald's Church, near Rufford. During the ceremony, when the priest asked if anyone present objected to the union of John Hargreaves and Mary Holt, members of the congregation were aware of the persistent sound of a baby crying somewhere nearby, yet no one could actually see a baby in the church. Then, gradually, a dark shadow materialised behind the kneeling couple, in the middle of the aisle. People seated at the front said it looked like the ghost of a frail girl. The mysterious figure wore a black veil which covered a chalk-white face and she seemed to be dressed all in black, clutching a crying baby in her arms.

John Hargreaves immediately seemed to recognise the gloomy spectre and his face paled. He was so terrified that he ran straight out of the church, causing the marriage service to be abandoned. At the same time, the congregation was shocked to see that the girl in black and her baby had also vanished, leaving no trace. The number of witnesses to this strange event was astonishing. About one hundred and thirty people claimed to have seen the ghostly lady.

Only one week later, John Hargreaves was found dead in his bed with a frozen look of absolute terror etched on his face. A servant claimed to have heard him screaming out at four o'clock that morning. Apparently the distraught man had been repeatedly shouting, "Leave me alone! Please, leave me alone!"

Dead Man Walking

In 1992, a farmer near Coppull in Chorley, telephoned the emergency services after seeing a car crash into a tree near a place called the Old Ring Mill. An ambulance sped to the scene, but the vehicle had skidded off the roadside and lay steaming in a ditch, just out of sight. Unable to find the vehicle, the ambulance pulled over cautiously in the driving rain and the paramedics rolled down the window to ask a passerby for directions.

The local man, dressed in blue overalls, pointed down a dark country lane but then turned to the driver and calmly announced with a doleful shake of his head, "If you're here to save the man trapped in the car, you're too late lads".

Eager to reach the victim as quickly as possible, the ambulance rushed off down the lane, screeching around the hairpin bend. There before them was the car, lying halfway into the ditch. It had impacted into a tree after skidding out of control. On further inspection, the paramedics found that the lone driver of the car lay inside the damaged vehicle. He was evidently dead from his injuries.

The ambulance-men shuddered as they realised that the dead motorist was wearing blue overalls, and they instantly recognised him as the local man who had just given them directions to the scene of the crash. He had warned them that they were too late, and it would seem that he had been right.

The deceased man had worked at a local garage and had been a popular and familiar face in the small village. After the tragic crash, on the following Thursday night at nine o'clock, eight drinkers in a local pub fell into stunned silence when the dead man walked in, right before their very eyes. Apparently he marched straight up to the bar and asked the barmaid for his usual drink. Needless to say, the girl fainted from the shock.

The dead man's friend stood up, obviously dumbfounded, and meekly asked him how on earth he could be present before them all. The man returned a puzzled stare before mournfully muttering, "I thought so; I thought I was dead." With that, he slowly turned and walked out of the pub. None of the bewildered drinkers had the courage to follow him, but two of them cautiously looked out of the window, only to find that there was absolutely no one there.

Apparently, the dead man made a few more ghostly appearances in the kitchen of his home and then again in a scrapyard, where he was spotted inspecting the wreckage of the car he had died in. Then he was seen no more.

Shopping Spectres

The two following stories are about ghost-like figures which haunted commercial premises.

This first story was related to me in February 2001. In the mid-1970s, there used to be a supermarket called the Bedford Stores situated near Bedford Street South, somewhere off Myrtle Street. One day, at around four o'clock, a stranger turned up in the supermarket dressed in old-fashioned clothes which looked as if they dated from the 18th century. He wore a tricorn hat (a traditional three-pointed hat) with a long, dark green coat down to his knees, tight white stockings and square-toed shoes with buckles on. The unusual man appeared to be aged about sixty-five, and he was wandering aimlessly around the supermarket aisles.

A witness, Mrs Carney, saw this odd figure up close and had thought that he was an actor taking part in some product promotion. The unusual figure had seemed apprehensive as he looked nervously about. Allegedly, the strange man had mumbled, in a very quaint accent, that he was lost. He was seen blundering about amongst the shelves of food by over ten shoppers, before disappearing completely.

A similar incident happened in 1968 at a shop called the Hat Box in Mount Pleasant, Liverpool. A man wearing a top hat and a long black coat came into the shop one rainy morning and inquired about a new topper. The shop assistant explained that they carried a range of top hats for weddings, and she nipped into the storage cupboard to look for the selection. When she returned shortly afterwards, the little shop was empty and the man had gone. The woman was confused because the bell on the door should have jangled if he had left the shop, so she began to feet extremely uneasy and cautiously searched the small premises in case he had hidden somewhere.

The boss of the Hat Box later told the curious shop assistant that the man in the top hat had turned up there just a few weeks earlier, and furthermore had vanished in front of her in the same way. Needless to say, the shop assistant ceased her employment at the shop abruptly!

When I related this mysterious incident on the *Billy Butler Show* on Radio Merseyside, eight separate people rang in and confirmed that the weird man had been sighted. One caller had worked at Walsby's Opticians near to the Hat Box. He distinctly remembered the top hatted gent from a bygone era occasionally passing by outside the Mount Pleasant premises.

Mona, the Cursèd Doll

Some people might laugh at the idea of a haunted doll, but I remember seeing Tony Hancock years ago in a television interview in which he said that when he was filming *The Punch and Judy Man*, he became convinced that the wooden Punch puppet he was using was evil. Hancock described how he had felt a powerful sense of evil emanating from the puppet and how everyone on the set knew there was something sinister about it. As the film was being made, the puppet master, Joe Hastings, suddenly died. Furthermore, when Hancock took the unusual Punch puppet home, his two dogs behaved completely out of character by relentlessly howling at it, before running away.

Here in Liverpool, there was another unlucky doll at large. She was called Mona, but 'Jonah' would have been more fitting! She was three feet long and had a mousey blonde crown of human hair with distinctive, strangely realistic-looking blue eyes. The doll's clothes were all black, a sinister colour for a child's toy!

The odd doll had been found abandoned in a barber's shop in Landford Avenue, near Sparrow Hall in 1959. No one ever turned up to claim it and so it was eventually given to a young girl named Elaine, who lived nearby in Wilbraham House, off Scotland Road. On the day on which she was given the doll, she was knocked down and killed instantly. Disturbingly, the darkly-clad doll was found lying on the ground near the body.

Elaine's mother was naturally devastated by the accident and felt even more upset by the sight of the funereal doll, which Elaine had named Mona, so she gave it to her niece, Jane, who lived in Belle Vale in one of the old prefabs. A week later, Jane's father was found dead. He was sitting in an armchair when he died, and at his feet lay the cursed doll. Jane's mother sensed there was something uncanny about the doll and threw it out. However, the travels of the terrible doll did not end there. Mona was found by a young child in the area. It seems that ill-fate followed the doll, because, shockingly, that child was later murdered, although for obvious reasons I cannot reveal any further details about who the young victim was.

In 1970, Jane's mother recoiled in horror when she spotted the unlucky doll in the window of a secondhand shop in Wavertree Road.

A week later, she was passing the same shop when she saw a woman and a child coming out of it. The child was grinning and hugging the evil doll, quite unaware of the terrifying trouble associated with it. It was later revealed that the mother and child lived in Janet Street. Apparently, within just one fortnight of purchasing the doll, the family suffered the loss of four relatives. The jinxed doll was allegedly last seen in Liverpool in 1979 at a primary school raffle.

Liberace's Haunted Candlesticks

In the late 1950s, the outlandish performer, Liberace, appeared at the Liverpool Show in Wavertree Park. At the end of his performance, he was chauffeured away in his Rolls Royce, followed by a convoy of trucks that carried his piano and other instruments. As the Rolls Royce was travelling up Wavertree High Street, Liberace ordered his chauffeur to pull over, because the performer's eye had just caught a glimpse of a number of interesting items in an antique shop near the corner of Sandown Lane. Liberace stepped out of the Rolls Royce as crowds of onlookers gathered round, and he went into the shop accompanied by his personal assistants. After a brief look round the shop, he purchased two large, solid silver candlesticks which dated back to the Regency Period, along with an old, gold-tinted mirror.

Liberace later placed the candlesticks on his favourite grand piano in his opulent Palm Springs villa. They complemented the unique, extravagantly-decorated piano which was encrusted with rhinestones, gold leaf and silvery mirrored sequins. Not long afterwards, peculiar things started to happen. One of Liberace's servants was about to retire one night after extinguishing all the candles, when she noticed that the lounge was still lit up. When the servant entered the room, she immediately saw that the candles in the silver candlesticks on the piano had been relit. She was confused by this because they had definitely been snuffed out earlier, and she was certain that she had seen no other person entering or leaving the lounge.

Another servant was awakened shortly afterwards when he heard someone hammering out Chopin's *Funeral March* on the piano at three o'clock in the morning. Liberace also heard the music and was furious at being awoken. He angrily flung back the bedcovers and leapt out of bed to see who was playing his piano at that unearthly hour. He was bemused to see a figure race past him, screaming out loud. It was the servant who had been disturbed by the music just moments earlier. By the light of the flickering candles, Liberace and another servant leant over to see nothing but a pair of ghostly pale hands playing his grand piano. Suddenly, the candles sputtered and the room was plunged into silent darkness.

This same weird scenario occurred again on the following night, so Liberace ordered the candlesticks to be packed up and he sent them back to the antique shop in Liverpool. After he had returned the candlesticks, the bizarre ghostly activity ceased and the nights were quiet once again at his villa.

Local legend has it that the silver candlesticks were often used for display purposes in the window of a Wavertree undertaker named McDougal. They had originally both rested on an old ornate coffin ...

Buyer Beware!

Older readers, cast your mind back a bit and you may remember the 'Maxi Mart' pages in the *Liverpool Echo*, where you could buy and sell quite a range of miscellaneous items, up to and including the kitchen sink! In February 1977, a Knotty Ash housewife named Chrissie Bradley, spotted a three-piece suite in beige vinyl advertised in the Household Goods column of the Maxi Mart. The three-piece suite was said to be in very good condition and the asking price was just £25. Chrissie phoned the man who was selling it, who said he would actually bring the three-piece suite himself to Chrissie's house, so she could see how good it was. The man, a Mr Posterway, duly turned up with the furniture and invited Chrissie to inspect it in the back of his transit van. When she saw the suite, she was very impressed and immediately agreed to pay Mr Postaway the asking price.

Not long after Chrissie had put the settee and two armchairs in her living room, weird things started to happen. Chrissie's twelve-year-old daughter was sitting on the settee one day, when she suddenly complained that her back felt damp. When she got up off the settee, the girl was horrified to discover that she had bloodstains on her white school shirt and ruby beads of blood were congealing on the settee.

Mr Bradley wiped down the stained material on the settee, but somehow the blood returned later on in the night. It was as if the settee was bleeding. Chrissie, distraught by the circumstances, telephoned Mr Postaway and asked him if he could explain why the settee was oozing the red sticky liquid. He refused to acknowledge what she was talking about and rudely hung up on her. Chrissie was unable to get through to him again after that, as he left his phone off the hook.

On the following day in the afternoon, Chrissie and her two friends were having a cup of tea, when the impression of a hand appeared on the beige vinyl of the settee. It looked as if someone had dipped his hand in blood, then pressed it onto the settee. Chrissie, disgusted, wiped the gruesome handprint with a cloth, but the stubborn mark returned later on. In the end, Mr Bradley thought there was something decidedly suspicious about the settee and he decided to dump it outside in the back alleyway, along with the two armchairs.

When the binmen arrived to remove the abandoned furniture, they saw pools of what looked like blood under the settee when they lifted it up onto the wagon. The ganger of the binmen was suspicious and he ripped the back of the settee open with a penknife, but the stuffing was as dry as a bone inside.

Years later, Chrissie Bradley learned that Mr Postaway had bought the settee from the wife of a woman whose husband had committed suicide on the sofa in 1972. The man had mistakenly thought he had cancer and in desperation had slashed his own throat as he lay on the sofa. The sofa had been cleaned and sold on, as the widow could not bear living with such a stark reminder of the fate of her dead husband. But the bloodstains kept reappearing on it. So, if you are thinking of purchasing something second-hand - buyer beware!

The Jonah Child

In the 19th century in Northern England, there were many alleged encounters with a strange young boy known as the 'Jonah Child'. The earliest reports of him date back to around the 1840s in Chester, where it was said that a red-headed ragamuffin child of about eleven or twelve years of age turned up in Chester. A family adopted the orphan, but they soon died in a terrible fire while he was out on an errand.

The boy, who gave his name as Gideon, was subsequently adopted by an elderly couple. Strangely enough, not long afterwards they also died, in this case from a fever. Gideon was adopted several more times and each family that took him under its wing met with a bad end or suffered some form of misfortune. As the rumours proliferated and spread about the so-called Jonah Child, he was driven out of the city and forced to wander the land in search of a family to care for him. The strange tales of the unlucky red-haired child circulated in England for decades, long after Gideon would have died from old age.

In August 1878, an elderly widow named Nancy Fellowes was shopping in Dale Street, when she saw a bare-footed child aged about twelve standing in a doorway. He had scruffy red hair and a dirty face and when the concerned lady enquired about his parents, he bluntly stated that he was an orphan. Mrs Fellowes was a religious woman and she felt a great deal of pity towards the street urchin. She hailed a hansom cab and took the child home to wash, clothe and feed him. He gave his name as Gideon, saying that he could not remember his surname because it had been so long since anyone had spoken it.

Gideon seemed to settle in well and was found a fairly well-paid job as a sack-maker at Twigg and Crosfield's flour and rice mill in Beaufort Street. On the first day of his new job, a fire of unknown origin burnt the mill to the ground. The damage was estimated at twenty thousand pounds. Stranger still, the very next day, Mrs Fellowes died suddenly of a stroke.

The cursed boy's tale did not end there. Mr Joseph Tate attended the same church as the late Mrs Fellowes and decided to act as a surrogate father to the orphan. The generous man took the boy into his home in south Liverpool. However, the very week that Gideon moved into his new home, Mr Tate's eight-year-old twin daughters suddenly became ill and later died from a mysterious illness. Tate suspected that Gideon was the carrier of the disease and immediately had him checked out by a physician, but the boy was found to be perfectly healthy.

Still tragedy continued to dog those who became associated with the rootless red-headed boy. One evening Mr Tate took Gideon to the Colosseum Theatre in Paradise Street. In the middle of the play, someone reported a burning smell in the theatre and there was a furious stampede out of the building. Thirty-seven people were trampled to death and Joseph Tate was severely injured. One of his crushed ribs pierced his lung, causing him to die a month later. Curiously, Gideon never suffered a scratch.

At this point, Tate's youngest sister, Louise, next took young Gideon under her wing. One misty morning in November of that year, she took the child to see the ships on the Mersey. As they reached the dock gates, an old blind Irish woman who was selling flowers reacted very strangely indeed as they approached. It was said that she had second sight and she was well-known in the area for her predictions and the uncanny way she could sense the true character of a person.

As Louise Tate approached her to buy some roses, the old woman shook her head and gestured for the girl to keep her distance. The blind flower seller made the sign of the cross and shouted, "If his shadow crosses your path, you won't have a minute's luck!"

At this odd remark, Gideon gave a little laugh and casually sauntered away. Louise followed after him, pensively reflecting over the old woman's strange words of warning. Literally minutes later, a dense fog rolled in. Before she knew it, Louise could see nothing at all. She shouted out for Gideon but only heard him laughing somewhere nearby. Then there was an almighty crash and heart-wrenching screams echoed from within the fog.

It happened that on the Mersey that day, the Seacombe ferry had collided with a sailing ship called the *Bowfell*. In the tragic collision an immense number of lives were lost.

Louise instinctively looked around for Gideon to make sure that he was safe but he was nowhere to be seen. Despite lengthy attempts to track him down, Louise Tate never found Gideon and many years later, she heard similar tales about other ill-fated people who had been unlucky enough to meet the so-called Jonah Child.

A Burns Night Ghost Story

As most people are aware, the evening of 25 January is celebrated in Scotland as Burns Night, in honour of Robbie Burns, the Scottish poet who was born on that date in 1759. Like the Welsh and the Irish, the Celtic history of the Scots abounds with ghost stories and tales of the supernatural. The following true story took place on Burns Night in Scotland, and was reported in the *Edinburgh Evening News*. The uncanny tale began, however, in a Liverpool pub ...

In January 1975, David McDonald, a Scottish bricklayer, was working on a building site in Liverpool city centre. During his lunch-break, he and his friend, Alec, went into the Caledonia pub in Catherine Street. It was there that he set eyes upon a beautiful nurse who worked across the road in the Women's Hospital. The nurse was called Maureen, and she was drinking with her friend, Iris, celebrating the fact that she was about to have a week off work.

David could not help overhearing the nurses' conversation and he and Alec went over to their table to ask if they could join them. The foursome got on like a house on fire. Soon, David plucked up the courage to ask Maureen if she had planned to go anywhere on her week off. Maureen coyly replied that she had not and David, with equal shyness, put forward a suggestion. He explained to her that his job in Liverpool would be ending in a few days and that he had planned to return home to visit his parents in West Lothian.

"Why don't you come up to Scotland with me to meet my parents? We can celebrate Burns Night together," he said, smiling broadly.

Maureen was not sure. After all, she had only just met the man. But, after meeting up again with David on the following night, she felt reassured and decided to accept his tempting offer.

A few days later, David and Maureen were travelling up to Scotland in his old Ford Cortina. David introduced Maureen to his parents, who took an immediate liking to the Liverpool girl. David decided that they needed some privacy, so when Burns' Night came, he decided to take Maureen to a remote West Lothian pub situated near the edge of a rugged stretch of heath. There was a full moon hanging in the sky which lent a romantic edge to the dusky evening, as Maureen and David walked hand in hand to the old pub, The Well, named after the old disused well that stood nearby.

The pub was cosy and welcoming with dark oak beams on the low ceilings, crossed Claymores over the fireplaces and clan tartans framed on the walls. It was obvious why the pub was so popular with the locals and the front bar was absolutely full to the brim. There was a narrow doorway to the side of the bar that led to a small snug parlour; in this detached room a blazing log fire crackled in the fireplace. The only person in there was a plump, round-faced man with silvery grey hair, who sat smoking his clay pipe, seemingly lost in an old book.

David yelled for the barmaid's attention over the hubub in the main bar and ordered two double whiskeys and a Hamlet cigar for himself. He then peeped back into the parlour. Spotting the chance for some peace and quiet and of grabbing a spare seat, he shouted over to the grey-haired gent, "Mind if we join you?"

The man looked up at David but did not respond. He just smiled and exhaled a cloud of pipe smoke which drifted up to the ceiling. David turned to the barmaid and curtly asked who the old guy was who was sitting in the parlour.

"Don't know," snapped the busy barmaid, without looking up.

"... the guy smoking the pipe. He's pig ignorant," David persisted.

"Smoking a pipe?" the barmaid asked, "Oh, that'll be Andy Erksine. He's a smug old reprobate. Take no notice of him."

David and Maureen entered the parlour and quickly kissed, before sitting down with their drinks in front of the blazing log fire. The old man looked the couple up and down with a sneer. David did not like his attitude at all, but tried to ignore him.

"Lovely pub," Maureen giggled. "A toast to Robbie Bruce!"

"Burns!" David laughed. "Robbie Burns, you Sassenach."

The old man sitting alone at the next table suddenly interrupted their banter.

"Robbie Burns. Aye, he was a character. Good old Robbie."

"Pardon?" David enquired, increasingly annoyed by the old man's rude manner.

There was no response, instead he abruptly turned in his seat, blanking David out. The peculiar old man then continued, addressing his speech to Maureen:

"Robbie disturbed a witch's coven not far from here about a hundred and fifty years ago. Jumped on his horse and rode for his life, but he just managed to escape, because his horse jumped over a stream as the witch was right behind him. Witches can't cross running water you see. If you believe all that."

Maureen smiled politely, but David saw an opportunity to wind the old man up.

"I certainly believe in the spirit world. This pub's haunted you know," he said, winking at Maureen.

The aged man puffed on his pipe and rigidly nodded in agreement. Maureen felt nervous as the talk turned to ghosts, she shivered and sipped her whiskey.

"You should have put lemonade in this," she complained, grimacing at the strength of the drink. David smirked and launched into his tale of the supernatural.

"About five years back I was in here with my brother Jimmy and his wife. You see that very poker there by the grate?"

Maureen and the old man simultaneously looked at the slightly bent iron poker hanging from a hook on the stone fire surround.

"Well, that poker started to sway like a pendulum. Backwards and forwards. Everyone saw it swinging. Then the temperature dropped. Everyone was shivering in here and yet the fire was blazing. It was really weird."

David became more carried away as he gleefully watched the worried look on Maureen's face.

"Oh stop talking about ghosts will you?" she said, realising that he was trying to wind her up but feeling increasingly uncomfortable nevertheless.

"It's Burns' Night, lassie; it's allowed," the old man retaliated. "It's traditional to talk about ghosties and ghoulies. This is one of the nights when they're allowed out of their cold graves to prowl about."

He then went on to relate a frightening story about a legendary black coach that was said to arrive outside the pub on dark winter nights such as this one. He said that all the curtains had to be tightly closed, because anyone who caught a glimpse of the coach would surely die soon afterwards.

David saw that Maureen was spellbound by the ghostly story and, becoming a bit jealous, he felt the need to compete.

"That's nothing, man. Not only did I see that poker move by itself that night, I also saw the ghost materialise in the corner over there."

"Oh shut up David, you're giving me the creeps," Maureen joked, grabbing his arm.

The old man paused.

"You actually saw the ghost?"

David nodded, holding the man's eye as he savoured a gentle sip of his Scotch whiskey, before continuing:

"Aye. He wore a Tam O'Shanter and a kilt. It was the tartan of the Campbells without a doubt."

"Nonsense!" shouted the old man loudly, with increasing

aggression.

David, satisfied with the reaction, got up to go to the toilet and smirked to himself.

"Just going to powder my nose," he told Maureen with a grin.

He swaggered out of the parlour, proud that he had topped the old man's tale.

Moments later when he returned, he found that the enclosed parlour had suddenly become crowded.

"What's going on?" he asked, shoving through the throngs of people. He then saw the barmaid leaning over Maureen and asking her if she was all right. The girl was exceptionally pale and her eyelids looked heavy, as if she was feeling faint.

"She fainted," the barmaid informed David.

Another drinker explained how he had heard the girl hit the floor with a thud.

"Maureen!" David cried, pushing his way through the crowd and grabbing her hand.

Maureen opened her eyes wide, "David! I want to go home!" and she began to sob softly.

"Calm down will you? What happened? Did the whiskey go to your head or something?"

David sat down next to her and put his arm around her. Maureen shook her head and started to tremble. She whispered with much fear in her voice:

"After you went to the toilet that, that - old man - he said you must have been lying about the ghost wearing the Campbells's tartan. He said that the ghost didn't wear a kilt at all," she whispered, with fear in her voice.

David was puzzled.

"Eh? What are you driving at?"

Maureen could hardly get her words out as her nerves got the better of her.

"David, that old man was the ghost," she gasped. "He just vanished right in front of me. I want to go home."

"He was never the ghost, Maureen. He was Andy. He's a regular here," said David reassuringly, looking up at the barmaid with a nervous grin.

The barmaid frowned, she shook her head and pointed to another old man sitting over the other side of the pub, puffing quietly on a pipe.

"No, that's Andy. I thought you were talking about him. He's the only pipe smoker I know of you see," she explained.

The crowd seemed very uneasy all of a sudden and filtered back to the bar, back to their drinks. David helped Maureen to her feet. As he assisted her on with her coat, she let out a piercing scream and froze, staring in horror at the fireplace. Although nobody was near it, the poker was swinging madly back and forth on its hook. Without a second's hesitation, David and Maureen literally ran out of that haunted pub without looking back.

Ghost researchers later discovered that an old pipe-smoking landlord named Alexander McCormick had been killed in the parlour of that pub in 1873. He had been tackling a burglar, who had clubbed him to death with a poker; the old man had been struck with such savagery that blood and brain tissue had splashed the walls and ceiling. Apparently, not long after the murder, that same poker was seen to rattle and sway of its own accord in the grate.

Sinister Effigies

Anyone who has ever visited Madame Tussaud's Waxwork Museum in London will have experienced the creepy feeling of being watched by the wax dummies as they walk in front of them. They are so cleverly and realistically formed that they appear to have a dark glimmer of life in their eyes as they stare straight ahead into the passing crowds.

The suspicion that wax effigies, or dolls, have a life of their own, probably stems from the fairy-tale way in which we thought about our toys as children, but, as ludicrous as it sounds, there have been unsettling accounts over the years of dolls, effigies and even statues moving as if they had a will of their own.

One day at noon, in the town of Quito in Ecuador, the congregation of a Catholic church was praying whilst staring intently at a statue of the Madonna. Suddenly, the statue of the Virgin Mary opened its eyes, looked directly at the kneeling supplicants and smiled. Most of the congregation fled in sheer terror; only one old woman and a young girl remained calm. Kneeling at the foot of the statue they were transfixed as the statue quietly blessed them with the sign of the cross, before glancing up at the crucifix on the altar and then turning back to stone again.

The authorities explained away the animated statue incident as the result of hysteria and religious mania, but the statue later became reanimated one afternoon when a botanical scientist was visiting the church, and although the scientist was a confirmed atheist, he signed an affidavit declaring that it had moved before his disbelieving eyes.

Of course, it is easy to dismiss such isolated cases in a distant rural South American town, but what about a window dummy that moved about in the dead of night in a shop situated in the sprawling metropolis of London? In the early 1970s, a boutique opened in North London called Fads. The shop had five window mannequins on display, and each morning, without fail, when the staff arrived and entered the premises, one specific dummy would be missing from its stand in the elaborate window display. Sometimes the dummy would be found on the second floor, or standing at the till behind the counter. This went on for some weeks and the antics of this dummy naturally became the source of much amusement at the boutique.

One of the proprietors, John Mikilson, who held a spare set of keys to the shop, was quickly accused of being the practical joker behind the dummy prank, despite his vehement protestations of innocence. The accusations were eventually put to an end when one weekend he was taken to hospital with appendicitis. The nurses took away his possessions which included his shop keys, his money and other valuables and locked them in the hospital safe while Mr Mikilson went under the knife to have his inflamed appendix removed. The other co-owner of the shop, Charles Meeker, locked up the boutique that Saturday afternoon. Then, while passing his boutique later, on the way to the tube station, he noticed that the restless window dummy was missing from the window yet again. This certainly unsettled him, as he could not blame Mr Mikilson this time.

Stranger still, one morning at around 1.30am, the police contacted Messrs Mikilson and Meeker because officers in a patrol car had spotted a woman walking about on the premises of Fads. The two shop owners drove to the shop and arranged to meet there with the police patrol car. The three policemen shone their torches at the strange figure in the window. It looked like a woman with red curly hair and a well-proportioned, almost perfect figure. However, when Mikilson, Meek and the policemen approached the window, they were all embarrassed to find that it was just a mannequin, which was now stationary.

The police were bewildered by the experience and quickly left the scene. A journalist from the *Evening Standard* wrote a piece on the bizarre case, giving all the details of the incident. This caused the police to complain that they were made to look like fools by the tone of the article. But as time moved on, the mysterious goings on were soon forgotten.

Fashions changed, and by 1974, the Fads boutique had folded and the contents of the store were sold on. The unruly dummy was sold to another clothes shop, however, as it was being delivered to the new store, the creepy mannequin was knocked to the ground while being carried into a van. The head fell off on impact. One of the workmen picked up the headless body and peered down the hole where the neck slotted in, he noticed what seemed to be some loose objects inside the drum of the dummy. He tipped it upside down and out fell a rabbit's-paw charm and a mummified frog of all things. As he shook the cask, out dropped an inverted cross, obviously a charm used by a Satan worshipper. More objects tumbled out of the dummy, including a scroll on which someone who was into black magic had written obscene sentences about the Devil conquering the world and destroying churches. No one ever discovered who gave the suspicious dummy to the boutique, or who owned the black magic paraphernalia, but when the newly-emptied dummy was used in the new boutique, it never wandered the store on its own again.

***

The following account is a really bizarre tale of another sinister effigy, and it is recorded in the annals of the, now-defunct, Lancashire Spiritualist Society. In 1955, small clay figures started to turn up on the doorstep of a Liverpool doctor. The little figurines were very elaborately made, with great attention to detail, and easily recognised as models of patients who had recently visited the doctor's surgery. One of the tiny, three inch figures was of a man in a cap; the doctor recognised that it was a model of a patient named Mr Bower, who suffered from a heart condition. On noticing that there was a long hat pin inserted directly into the clay figure's chest, the doctor shook his head, dismissing it as some prank by a complete joker with a penchant for voodoo.

However, less than one hour after receiving the bizarre doll, the doctor received a telephone call informing him that Mr Bower had suffered a massive heart attack. Furthermore, he had died at the precise time when the doctor had found Bower's effigy. Three more clay figures turned up, and there were three more corresponding deaths, seriously unsettling the doctor.

One morning, the doctor turned up at his surgery earlier than usual. As he fumbled to lock his car door, he looked up to notice a suspicious figure hovering near his door. It was clearly the mystery depositor, so the doctor quickly made his way over. To his disgust, the figure was leaning down over the step, placing more of the sinister figures there. He angrily reached out to touch the malevolent prankster, only to discover that it was a young attractive woman of about twenty-five. The doctor recognised her immediately as a past patient who had made sexual advances towards him during a consultation several months back. The doctor, a happily married man, had refused the forceful young lady, totally rejecting her sexual overtures. It occurred to him that the dolls seemed to be part of some bizarre revenge scheme.

On being caught in the act, the woman had blushed excessively and fled in shame before the doctor got a chance to catch her. After checking the woman's records, the doctor remained concerned and later visited her home, in the Kensington district of Liverpool. There, he learned that the woman and her mother had set about avenging the girl's rejection; they were both obsessed with the occult and had used it as a means to manipulate events. The doctor was more than a little concerned about the mental health of the woman, who was obviously unbalanced, and so he arranged for a local priest to visit her. From that day onwards no more clay figures turned up on the steps of the doctor's surgery!

A Hair-Raising Experience

In the summer of 1996, *The Times* newspaper, which isn't exactly renowned for its offbeat stories, ran a report about a bizarre phenomenon that was taking place in Madame Tussaud's Waxworks.

A number of maintenance staff at the waxworks noticed that the dummy of Adolf Hitler suddenly needed a haircut. It seemed that the Fuhrer's fringe had actually somehow grown three centimetres. The dummy was removed from its glass display cabinet and the tabloids had a field day as the staff at Madame Tussaud's consulted a trichologist from Leeds to analyse the dummy's hair, which happened to have been imported from Germany.

The hair expert had to admit that she was baffled by the phenomenon. She could not explain how Hitler's hair could possibly be growing. Two months later, the dummy's hair suddenly stopped growing, just as mysteriously as it had started. The dummy of Adolf Hitler had been modelled from the Austrian dictator while he was still alive in the 1940s and, over the years, many visitors have claimed that the sinister dummy's eyes have a look of pure evil in them. Some have even claimed that they saw them move!

The Harrowing Harmonica

In the early 1970s, a wax museum was opened in Long Beach Amusement Park in Los Angeles. It had not been open long when all sorts of weird things began to happen. Lights would switch on and off in the middle of the night, without cause or explanation and the sounds of footsteps would echo through the empty building in the dead of night when the security guards were stationary and not patrolling the corridors. Again, there seemed to be no explanation.

At 2.30am one morning, Steve Jackson, a security officer, heard the distinctive sound of someone playing the harmonica somewhere down in the Wild West section of the museum. The guard slipped his gun from its holster and crept downstairs with his flashlight, prepared to confront the intruder. He passed the wax dummies of Jessie James, Pat Garret, Billy the Kid and Doc Holliday. The guard began to feel that he was being taunted, as the sound of the mouth organ grew louder. As soon as the beam of the his flashlight scanned one particular wax dummy in the corner, the ghostly harmonica stopped playing. Jackson switched on the lights and radioed the other guard on the top floor of the building to come down to help him to corner the intruder.

The other guard had also heard the faint strains of the harmonica in the early hours of the morning on several occasions, but had never mentioned it to anyone. As the two guards closed in and surrounded the model, they were surprised to find that there was nobody there, and no one had passed by them either. Jackson took a closer look at the cowboy in the corner, which was propped up against a mockup of a saloon bar. The figure was diminutive, about five foot one, which was unusual because most of the gunfighter dummies were fashioned to be much taller and larger than life by the figure-makers, purely for dramatic effect.

The cowboy had a sad expression and wore a droopy moustache. The inquisitive guard leaned closer to read the plate next to the exhibit, which revealed that his name was Elmer J McCurdy, an outlaw who had been shot to death after a failed train robbery in 1911. Both of the guards agreed that this wax figure's eyes were chillingly life-like. He had a piercing, sinister stare, quite unlike the other dummies.

About a year later, in 1976, a segment of the popular American TV series, *The Six Million Dollar Man*, starring Lee Majors, was being filmed in the Long Beach Amusement Park and some scenes were actually shot in the Wild West section of the museum. During the filming of a dramatic fight scene, an actor, battling away with Lee Majors, accidentally stumbled and knocked over the wax dummy of Elmer McCurdy. When the dummy hit the floor, the impact caused both its arms to fall off and the horrified actors and film crew then saw that the damaged figure was not a dummy at all, it was a mummified person. Fragments of bone, dried skin and blood were scattered on the floor, making the onlookers feel physically sick.

The police investigated the matter and discovered that, in 1911, the body of the outlaw, Elmer McCurdy, had been taken down from the gallows and preserved by embalming, before then being given a coating of wax. This practice was not uncommon in America at that time and many notorious criminals were preserved in this ghoulish way for public display at carnivals and shows. The proprietors of the Los Angeles museum had bought the waxwork figure without enquiring about its origins and were staggered to discover that it was in fact a real corpse. After Elmer McCurdy was taken from the museum and given a formal burial, the spooky goings on ended and the harmonica was never heard again.

The Laughing Lady

In October 2000, Colin and Shirley, a couple in their late sixties, moved into a house in the Devonshire Park area of Wirral. Their new neighbours seemed to be an unusually quiet lot, and Shirley had a sneaking suspicion that their silence had something to do with the house that they had just moved into. Colin, a pragmatic and down-to-earth sort of man, thought the neighbours were simply snobby and stand-offish, but Shirley, who had maintained that she was partly psychic for years, became increasingly convinced that the old Edwardian dwelling, which they intended to make into their home, had some supernatural aura about it.

Appropriately, it was on the night of Halloween when Shirley and Colin had their first skirmish with the ghostly goings on of the house. They were sitting in the living room, watching a soap opera on the television, when Colin suddenly heard a noise.

"What's that?" he said, with slight concern in his voice.

"What?" Shirley asked, and turned down the volume on the remote control. In the now silent room she also heard the distinct sound of running footsteps pattering noisily up and down the stairs of the house. Colin grabbed an old poker from the empty grate and told Shirley to stay put. He strode into the hall and gazed up the stairs into the darkness of the upstairs landing. The thumping footfalls on the carpeted staircase grew considerably louder, until it sounded as if someone was heading straight towards Colin. He braced himself for the intruder to show himself.

Then, to his amazement, a woman in black appeared at the stop of the stairs. Not a woman of today, but obviously someone out of another century, for the clothes she wore looked dowdy and Victorian. The puffed-sleeved blouse she wore was ebony black with a dull sheen, and the bell-shaped, ankle-length dress was equally dreary. The strange female had a ghastly, ashen face with large, black, unblinking eyes. Her quaint mouth was curled into a subtle smile. As Colin was nervously mouthing the question, "Who are you?", the woman vanished. According to Colin, she literally 'just went', and as she did so, he distinctly felt a cool breeze brush against his cheek.

He slowly turned round to see Shirley framed in the doorway to the living room with her hand to her mouth. Her blue eyes were transfixed on the spot where the phantom had stood before dematerialising. She had obviously also seen it.

The couple were extremely unsettled by what they had seen and felt very uncomfortable in their new house. They decided to consult a medium. Unfortunately, he was one of the many unscrupulous fakes who prey on the gullible in society, including the desperate people who have traumatically discovered that their homes have unwanted spiritual inhabitants.

Immediately on reaching the house, the so-called medium claimed that he detected the spirit of a woman who had died in there in the 1950s. This apparition, he confidently asserted, had come out of 'a sort of suspended animation period in Limbo' because Colin had rewired the house recently. He explained that the electrical activity had caused the apparition to be powered up. The medium charged the couple an extortionate sum of money, and then set about discharging the resurrected spirit with what he called 'white cleansing candles', which were placed at various points around the house.

Of course, this clap-trap was completely ineffective, as Shirley found out to her horror a week later. On this particular evening, Colin had gone out for the night with two friends. Shirley's friend from Liverpool had promised to stay with her for a few hours, but had not turned up for some reason. Shirley had just conjured up enough guts to go up the sinister staircase to turn a heater on in the bedroom, when the lights dimmed on the stairs.

What happened next completely overwhelmed her. The outdated lady who had appeared weeks before, quite literally came flying towards her down the stairs. The ghost's arms were outstretched and her feet pointed upwards at a 45-degree angle. The figure was screeching with laughter as she flitted straight towards Shirley, who was paralysed with shock. The figure in black dramatically twisted away just before she reached her, and then flew past her down the next flight of steps. Shirley was petrified and sank to her knees, feeling sharp, stabbing pains in her chest. She could scarcely breathe, she felt so weak with the terror. Suddenly, the sound of hysterical laughter ceased, as the lights on the stairs simultaneously returned to their normal luminance.

At around 11.45pm, Colin returned from his night out playing snooker with his friends and found all the lights on in the house and

Shirley trembling under the duvet of their bed. She related the spine-chilling experience she had endured earlier, and Colin took her downstairs for a coffee. He had given up cigarettes as a Millennium resolution in December 1999, but now he had an uncontrollable urge to light up. Earlier that night when he had told his friends about the ghost in his home they had just laughed. Colin did not know who to turn to and they seriously considered moving out of the accursed house. That was just before he telephoned me at Radio Merseyside after hearing me on the *Billy Butler Show*. On hearing the traumatic story, I told him I would come out to have a look at the house and hopefully uncover something about the ghostly occupant by leafing through the old electoral registers.

The day before I arrived, another spectacular occurrence took place at that dreaded house in Devonshire Park. At around midnight, Colin and Shirley were dozing off on their sofa, as they watched a late-night film on the television. A sudden sound, which came from the hallway, woke Shirley up. It sounded like the brass letterbox flap opening. Shirley shivered with fear; she prodded Colin and alerted him to the persistent noise. He grabbed a heavy ornamental candlestick from a display cabinet and crept across the living room towards the door. The only light in the room came from a small, ruby-coloured lampshade in the corner. Colin was about to switch on the main light, but decided against it, because if someone was attempting to break into the house, the less they saw of him the better.

He gently pulled the door open by a few degrees and peeped into the hallway. A long pole was protruding from the open letterbox. It had a hook on the end and its shaft was embedded with razor blades. Colin realised that a criminal outside was attempting to snatch his car keys, which were lying on a table in the hallway. If Colin attempted to seize the pole, the blades on it would slice through his hands as the crook outside retracted it.

Shirley came up behind Colin and asked, in a whisper, what was going on, but she was pushed back into the living room. He grabbed his mobile phone from the coffee table and started to dial 999, when he heard a voice yell out. Screams came from his doorstep and a loud rattling sound echoed in the hallway.

Colin ran to the bay window and pulled aside the curtain. There was a shaven-headed youth on the doorstep and he was staring in horror at his hands, which were dripping with blood. The end of the pole he had been holding was violently thrusting backwards and forwards through the letterbox. Colin immediately wondered who could possibly shoving and pulling the deadly pole from inside his hallway. As he watched, the youth stumbled away with blood pouring copiously from his hands, clearly in a state of complete shock. The pole then shot back into the house through the letterbox and landed with a clatter in the hallway. The youth shot a puzzled glance at Colin through the window, before running off holding his crimson hands under his arms. Colin only snapped out of his confusion when he heard a tinny-sounding voice coming from his phone, asking which emergency service he required.

When the police arrived, they took a look at the pole with the hook and razor blades lying in the hallway. They had seen such poles before and knew that their purpose was to obtain keys, or anything else left within reach in hallways. This pole was bloodstained, but Colin said he was at a loss to explain who had been able to pull the pole out of the criminal's hands. That same person had possessed the strength to ram the bladed pole back at the would-be thief, lacerating his hands.

Shirley had her own theory. She believed it had been the ghost of the house. After all, who else could it have been? It wasn't as if the youth had had an accomplice who had turned on him. The young scally had almost definitely been alone.

When I looked into the case, I found that the house did have strange cold spots. To investigate further, I left a tape recorder with various special microphones fitted to it. One microphone was a transducer that can pick up sounds in the ultrasonic range, and it was this microphone which detected a faint laughing sound. There was also a curious message spoken by a young female voice which clearly stated the words, 'Rosalind isn't mad!'

On the following day I scoured through the electoral registers and discovered that a woman named Rosalind Lundy had once lived at the haunted house. Alas, as I was continuing my research into the elusive Rosalind, Colin and Shirley's nerves could endure no further middle-of-the-night visitations from the laughing lady, and they moved away to St Michael's Hamlet in Liverpool.

To date, the house in Devonshire Park is empty, except of course for the troubled vestige of a woman of long ago.

Terrifying Time-slips

Mirage of Mass Murder

This is a really uncanny story which was reported to me back in the 1980s. One blistering sunny afternoon in May 1981, two American children and their Liverpool-born grandfather were enjoying the summer weather on the coast of Cork, near a beautiful stretch of coastline known as the Old Head of Kinsale. Seven-year-old Aaron Fitzpatrick and his six-year-old sister, Siobhan, played energetically as their grandfather relaxed back into his deckchair to soak up the sun. As he snoozed, he was calmed by the comforting sound of the children giggling as they ran along the beach, throwing a frisbee to each other.

At ten minutes past two that afternoon, the sleeping grandfather was roughly shaken out of his pleasant snooze as Aaron and Siobhan almost pushed him out of his deckchair. With shrieks of laughter, they excitedly tried to wake him up.

"What in God's name?" he cried out, feeling confused as he sat himself forward in his chair.

The giddy children pointed enthusiastically to the strange spectacle that was unfolding in the waters off the coast.

About a mile or so out, an enormous liner resembling the *Titanic* was listing heavily to starboard, sinking nose-first. A long plume of black smoke was rising from the stricken vessel and there was a muffled din coming from the direction of the sinking liner. With a mounting sense of horror, the children's grandfather realised that the unruly clamour was actually the distorted screams of what sounded like a thousand or more people. As he squinted, he could just about make out some figures that appeared like dots in the waters surrounding the rapidly-sinking ship.

Little Siobhan looked up at her grandfather and enquired curiously, "What's wrong with that boat, Grandad?"

Just as he was attempting to rationalise the ghastly vision before them, it disappeared - within the blinking of an eye, there was no longer any sign of a sinking ship, or of any passengers, or lifeboats in the water. All that could be made out on the horizon was a flock of seagulls, blithely skimming across the waves. The screams had also ceased, just as abruptly.

Despite the heat of the summer afternoon, the Liverpudlian grandfather felt an immensely cold chill creeping through his bones.

As he stood scratching his head in confusion, he slowly recalled the date, 7 May. On that very date in 1915, during the First World War, the Cunard liner, *Lusitania,* had been torpedoed by a German submarine in that very same stretch of water. The ship had been on her way to Liverpool from New York when she was suddenly attacked. A staggering 1,198 people perished in the awful disaster, which was branded afterwards as nothing short of a brutal act of mass murder.

As the grandfather guided the bemused children away from the beach, little Siobhan's curiosity was still unsatisfied and she asked what had become of the ship. Her grandfather sighed and pensively scanned the horizon.

"Oh, it's long gone down," he replied distantly.

In fact, the *Lusitania* had gone to a watery grave sixty-six years before. What they had just witnessed seemed beyond reality, some ghostly replay, or tragic mirage, from another era.

A Stroll into Limbo

The following eerie story came to my attention in December 2000, when a retired priest telephoned me at the studios of BBC Radio Merseyside. I went along to interview him and he seemed very sincere. I have had to change a few names to abide by the priest's request for anonymity.

In December 1986, two Catholic priests came out of the Diocesan Council Office on Brownlow Hill at about five minutes to five in the afternoon. Father Howard was the older priest and Father Andrew was just twenty-five. As they walked up the street on their way to a bookshop called Parry's Books, they suddenly noticed that things were unusually quiet. Not a single person passed them and there were no cars on the road at all, even though it was the middle of rush hour.

The priests walked into the bookshop on Brownlow Hill and found the place deserted as well. The cash registers were operational and the place was lit up, yet there was no one else about. Not a single member of staff or a customer could be seen. This obviously made the priests uneasy. They waited and waited, but no one came into the place and there was no one outside to be seen either. Father Andrews nervously joked, "Perhaps there's a bomb scare on and everyone's been evacuated!"

The other priest only frowned.

The time seemed to drag by and when Father Howard glanced out of the bookshop window at the University clocktower, he was amazed to see that the time was still five minutes to five. It was almost as if time itself was standing still. Father Andrew was becoming increasingly agitated so he tapped on the door of the bookshop staffroom, but there was no answer. When he looked inside, he saw handbags and coats and other items belonging to the staff, but no sign whatsoever of anyone. It was a scene more reminiscent of the *Mary Celeste* than of a normally-busy city centre bookshop.

According to Father Andrews, the baffled priests went next door to a pub called the Augustus John where, to their horror, they found the premises to be equally deserted. The one-armed bandits were illuminated and the bar and lounge were lit up, yet no one was about.

Feeling more and more disconcerted and perplexed, the two priests decided to hurry back to the Diocesan Council building on Brownlow Hill.

"I don't like this one little bit," Father Andrew whispered to his colleague, halfway through the journey.

"I think it's 'the other fella', up to his tricks," replied Father Howard, flickering his eyes downwards in a knowing way.

Young Father Andrews knew exactly to whom he was referring - the Devil.

"Jesus, please get us out of this situation," murmured Father Howard, reverently.

At that precise moment, a vagrant, who was well known in the area, ambled round the corner from the direction of the Students' Union building. The next thing that the two priests heard was the screeching sound of a bus's pneumatic brakes. When they turned around, there was the usual heavy traffic on Brownlow Hill again. Then they heard the clocktower striking five o'clock.

The priest who recited this strange incident to me showed me his old diary for December 1986 and there was the full account written down, exactly as he had told it to me. The other priest, who is now working in London, also confirmed the weird story.

"It was as if we had strolled into Limbo that day," Father Howard had reflected with a shudder.

Tricky Timing

The following strange story was related to me by a local retired policeman. For reasons that will shortly become clear, I have had to change a few names and details.

In December 1960, Sid, a 55-year-old Liverpool man, chose to break into a garage in Catherine Street, not far from the site of the old Women's Hospital. He was aware that the manager always left the week's takings in a strong box in his office; the money was there for the taking. At around a quarter to twelve, Sid climbed up a drainpipe and managed to clamber onto the garage roof. As he started to prise the skylight window open with a small jemmy crowbar, he cursed as it started to snow with enormous, wet snowflakes. The skylight frame would not budge, and the roof was becoming treacherous because of the slushy snowfall.

Suddenly, a blinding light flashed up into Sid's eyes; he had been spotted by a suspicious policeman down in the street below. The thief panicked and tottering unsteadily across the roof-tops, he climbed onto the roof of the Ritz Roller Skating Rink, which was situated on the corner of Myrtle Street. Incidentally, this place later became known as the Rodney Youth Centre.

As a police car arrived at the disturbance down in the street, Sid used the crowbar to smash a roof-top window pane and slid into the building. He stumbled over some randomly strewn objects in the pitch black loft, as he tried to make his way out, before clumsily pulling the hatch up and dropping down into a deserted corridor.

Sid gradually realised that it probably would not be long before he was caught; he sweated profusely and desperately wracked his brains to find an escape route. He became aware of the echoing sound of distant music playing somewhere downstairs in the roller-skating rink. He cautiously crept down the steps and opened the doors. What he then saw would haunt him for the rest of his life. Instead of a skating rink, before him was a large hall with huge, elaborate, crystal chandeliers suspended from the ornate ceiling. Couples were waltzing about in the grand hall, all dressed in noticeably old-fashioned clothes. The women wore long, bell-shaped dresses and elegant head dresses and the men were dressed in long black coats with 'hammer' tails. Bright Christmas decorations and garlands were attractively strung around the walls and at the far end of the hall, a small orchestra was playing.

Sid assumed that some fancy dress ball was in progress and decided it would be an ideal means of escape to mingle in amongst the people and so hide from the police. However, when the dancers saw Sid enter the dance hall, they stopped waltzing and the music gradually died down. In a quaint Lancashire accent, a ruddy-cheeked man with white side-whiskers demanded to know exactly who he was. The crafty criminal gave a false name as his eyes greedily drifted over to a huge table which was laden with bottles of wine and punch. Cheekily, and stupidly, since he was supposed to be keeping a low profile, he asked for a drink, but was flatly refused.

Sid was suddenly grabbed by his collar and escorted roughly out of the hall. As he attempted to resist the forceful man, he glanced back and saw that all the chandeliers were growing rapidly dimmer, until everything became absolutely pitch black. He felt the man release his grip on his collar and then realised that he was completely alone in the roller-skating rink. He was so thrown off balance by the whole unbelievably uncanny incident, that he banged on the front doors of the building and yelled for help. The police rapidly gained entrance to the skating rink, to be confronted by Sid in a terrible state. He literally ran into their arms and stuttered out what had just happened.

Sid was well known to the police and certainly was not renowned for having flights of fancy and imagination; to his dying day he swore that he had somehow stumbled upon a Christmas ball of long ago, right there in the Ritz Roller Skating Rink in Catherine Street.

Incidents such as the aforementioned suggest that all time and all events of past, present and future are eternally present, but stretched out along a dimension we cannot yet properly access or visualise. A good analogy is a compact disc containing say, the works of Mozart. What we call 'now' is the position of the laser stylus as it plays the present parts of the current track. Yet, the other tracks are also present on the disc, but the stylus has either passed them, or has not quite reached them yet, either way those tracks are still there.

Now, imagine the events of your life from birth to death all set out in time like the tracks on a CD. Where you are now, the present, is merely where the stylus is. Perhaps if the stylus jumped you would experience déjà vu. If this theory is correct, then, as you read these words, Moses is on his way to the mountain, Booth has just shot Lincoln and the first human being has just set foot on Mars.

On a more personal level, you have just taken your first breath after being delivered, you are holding this book and you have just been buried! Sobering thoughts.

Back to the Future

In 1970, 10-year-old Sarah Jones was going on an errand near Sugar Lane in Knowsley, when she saw a very curious sight. She spotted her mother coming down the lane, a quite normal experience, except for the fact that her mother looked very strange indeed. Her hair had been cut very short and she was wearing an extremely funny-looking one-piece suit with what looked like chunky white pumps. Sarah was baffled because she knew her mother was at work, so, intrigued, she shouted, "Mum!" across the road to her. Her mother did not even glance over, as she paused by a window before walking on down the lane and disappearing out of sight round a corner.

At five o'clock that evening Sarah's mother returned home as usual. She looked the same as she always did, and much to her daughter's surprise, she had not had her hair cut. Sarah became excited and eagerly explained to her mother that she had seen her exact double who had short hair and wore funny clothes, but Mrs Jones was tired and took hardly any notice of her daughter's chatter.

That same week, Sarah Jones wrote down a detailed account of the strange encounter with her mother's double in her English exercise book. The English teacher praised her for the piece, saying it had been a very vivid and imaginative story. Little did Sarah know that the childish account was to become necessary proof of the scenario in years to come.

Some twenty years later, Sarah Jones, at the age of thirty, was walking down Sugar Lane when she glanced at her reflection in a window. She stopped dead in her tracks. That specific incident from her childhood instantly flashed into her mind. There, reflecting back at her, was the identical figure she had passed all those years ago. After all, the Sarah Jones of 1990 had short hair and the one piece suit she wore was a shell-suit, accompanied by a new pair of white Nike trainers. Her recollection of that woman, whom she had seen in 1970, she now realised had not been her mother, or a double. The young Sarah Jones had somehow seen a preview of her future self, twenty years away.

Coincidentally, there have been a number of other timeslips in that area which will one day be the subject of an incredible future story. In one present day case, dozens of people heard a low droning sound in the sky and when they looked up, they saw a formation of strange aeroplanes. Seconds later the planes had disappeared. A man in Prescot who had managed to catch a glimpse of the phantom planes with binoculars confirmed that they had been World War Two German bombers. How could that have been possible?

Miracles

The Mysterious Nun

In 1964, a sixty-year-old Everton man named Patrick O'Rourke was working for Martindales, a coal firm. He was humping a heavy bag of coal up several flights of steps to the fourth landing of a tenement block off Brownlow Hill, the Bullring Tenements to be precise. As he struggled up the steep staircase, he suddenly felt overwhelmingly dizzy. He collapsed on the stairs, where one of the residents, a Mrs Scott, found him lying semi-conscious, clutching a medal which depicted the Blessed Virgin Mary. The other coalmen rushed up to the landing and carried him down to the coal-lorry and then quickly drove him to the Royal Liverpool Hospital.

He had suffered a severe stroke and things looked extremely bleak. Mrs O'Rourke and her family crowded into the ward where her husband lay dying. Surrounding his bed, they all prayed fervently for his recovery. Dr Bosankay, who had been treating Mr O'Rourke, advised his distressed wife to go home that night, as there was nothing she could do at the hospital. But the woman begged the doctor to allow her and her eldest daughter to stay, which he cautiously allowed.

At 3am that morning, Patrick O'Rourke's breathing became shallow and laboured and then ceased altogether; his wife and daughter began to sob hysterically as his life ebbed away. In deep emotional turmoil, they were suddenly startled as an unfamiliar nun entered the room unannounced.

"Don't cry," she calmly urged them, before silently gliding round the side of the bed.

She reached out and clutched Mr O'Rourke's hand.

"Thank you, sister," Mrs O'Rourke stammered, choking back the tears.

As she hugged her daughter she felt desperately sad, but somewhat comforted by the presence of the reassuring nun.

It was at that moment that Mr O'Rourke suddenly opened his eyes. He looked first at the nun's kind face and then turned to his wife and daughter.

"What are you crying for?" he innocently asked, before complaining of a terrible thirst.

Mrs O'Rourke and her daughter flung their arms about his neck and smothered him with kisses. Then, overwhelmed with joy, they turned to thank the nun, whom they were convinced was somehow responsible for his miraculous recovery, only to find that the ward was empty once more. Mrs O'Rourke apologised for the commotion they were making as an elderly patient in the ward stirred in his sleep and then woke up. He shook his head, dismissing her apology with sympathetic understanding. The relieved wife could not contain herself and felt the urge to tell someone about the kindly nun who had seemingly revived her husband and brought him back from the brink of death. She began to tell the old man about the miraculous events which had just taken place and about the nun's involvement in his recovery.

"She's a ghost," the old man interrupted her, in a deadly serious tone.

He explained that the nun had been seen on other occasions in the Royal Liverpool and other local hospitals. Apparently she was well known amongst the patients and sometimes gave her name as Veronica.

Mrs O'Rourke was intrigued by the tale and later on that week she mentioned the mysterious nun to Dr Bosankay. At the mere mention of the nun's involvement he turned pale. He seemed lost for words, before then saying that no nuns worked in the hospital, especially at three o'clock in the morning. He nevertheless admitted that he and his colleagues were completely baffled by Patrick O'Rourke's amazing recovery. Even after keeping him in for observation, he simply could not explain his sudden and total recovery.

That same week, Mrs O'Rourke told her parish priest about the strange incident. He did not seem to be at all alarmed by the claim and revealed to her that a nun had also recently appeared to a child in the Children's Hospital in Myrtle Street. That child had miraculously recovered from life-threatening meningitis overnight. Apparently, the nun had also been seen by a night nurse who had heard the angelic-looking woman actually identify herself as Sister Veronica. There were rumours that the same phantom nun had been encountered at the Notre Dame Convent in Hope Street, many years before.

In 1965, a mysterious nun also appeared at a house in Bromborough, where a Mrs Durban was giving birth. After a long and difficult labour, a healthy baby girl was finally born. However, the mother faded rapidly after the delivery and then lost consciousness. The midwife was seriously concerned and rushed to telephone for an ambulance. When she returned to the bedroom, she found a willowy nun leaning over Mrs Durban. An anxious-looking Mr Durban was holding his wife's hand, repeatedly whispering, "There's no pulse".

The midwife was mystified by the nun's sudden appearance and asked her how she had got into the house, but received no reply. The nun just silently put the palms of her hands on each side of Mrs Durban's face and started to whisper a melodious prayer. Mr Durban later reported that he distinctly remembered the nun uttering something about Saint Anthony.

About a minute later, Mr Durban felt a weak fluttering in his wife's wrist - her pulse had returned! As he hugged her tightly she faintly murmured the words, "I want to come back to see my baby". Her husband then became slightly alarmed, because he claimed that, at that moment, the nun's face had seemed to radiate a startling golden light.

Mrs Durban regained full consciousness in a cold, clammy sweat, still in the comforting embrace of her husband. The ambulance arrived at that moment and, in the confusion, no one saw the obscure nun leave. The ambulance-men stated that they had seen no one pass them on the path outside, even though that was the only way the nun could have left the premises. So, was the ethereal nun actually a ghost and could she have been the mysterious Veronica?

Miracle on Sandy Road

This is a strange but true tale about a miracle that is alleged to have taken place at Seaforth in 1935.

John and Catherine Crosse lived at a house in Seaforth's Sandy Road. The couple had just one child, a three-year-old daughter named Rosy. As they were both ardent atheists, they had consciously chosen not to tell little Rosy about God, or religion, and there was not so much as a copy of the Bible to be found anywhere in the house.

John and Catherine Crosse had a tempestuous relationship and were always having heated rows. On more than one occasion, the neighbours had to intervene when the domestic trouble got out of hand. Rosy often became distressed when she overheard her argumentative parents and would usually hide under the stairs whenever they began rowing. She was brought up with strict discipline and was often punished for unnecessarily crying by being locked away in her bedroom.

One specific night, Rosy had been locked in her room and her parents were arguing as usual, when they suddenly heard cries coming from upstairs. It turned out that Mr Crosse had carelessly left his pipe on his bed and a fire had subsequently broken out. The fire spread rapidly and when Mrs Crosse opened the bedroom door, clouds of thick black smoke billowed out and a blast of fierce heat drove them both back.

Mr Crosse searched desperately for the key to Rosy's bedroom, but could not find it in the ensuing panic. Amidst the mad search, the blaze upstairs spread rapidly and the smoke finally forced the couple downstairs.

Mr Crosse was distraught and dashed round to a neighbour's house. Borrowing his ladder, he then tried to climb up to reach the window of Rosy's bedroom where he could hear his little girl crying. Mrs Crosse was hysterical by now and a crowd had assembled in the street. They too heard the child's cries and became increasingly anxious for her safety. A few people claimed that they actually saw Rosy's little terror-stricken face peering through the soot-coated windows.

As the crowd grew, an old woman from the next street made her way down the road. She pushed through the bystanders and made her way up to Mrs Crosse, who was weak with fear. The old woman reassured her that her daughter was completely safe. As Mrs Crosse tearfully looked up at her, the woman calmly reiterated that Rosy was just across the way in her garden. Mr Crosse, stressed to breaking point by the entire scenario, snapped back at her, saying that the old woman was mistaken. However, when the fire brigade finally put the fire out, they found that Rosy's bedroom was empty.

The old woman once again insisted that the child was in her garden, so Mr and Mrs Crosse, completely dazed, went to see if she was telling the truth. Evidently she was; there sat Rosy, playing away happily in the woman's tiny back garden. When the couple saw her, they both grabbed at the little girl and hugged her. But how on earth had she escaped from that locked room?

When questioned by her concerned mother, Rosy explained that a man had taken her away from her room. The girl was so young that she did not have the vocabulary to describe coherently exactly what had happened. Her parents did not push the issue further, filled with relief that their daughter was safe and well. As they left the kind old woman's house, Rosy suddenly stopped in her tracks and yelped happily as she put her hand to her mouth.

"What's the matter, Rosy?" Mrs Crosse asked.

Rosy pointed her little finger at something on the wall. It was a picture of Jesus, the picture often referred to as, 'The Sacred Heart'.

"That man, mummy," the little girl announced and continued to babble incoherently as a child of that age often does. Rosy's mother knelt down, looked her straight in the face, and listened carefully to her little girl.

"That man came and took me, mummy," said Rosy, so clearly that there could be no mistake.

Later that week, when the girl was given some crayons, she even drew the mysterious man who had saved her life. The childish scribbles depicted the archetypal religious image of a man with a beard dressed in a long robe.

Funnily enough, after the extraordinary experience, Rosy's parents altered their atheistic views and became dedicated church-goers. News of the strange incident somehow reached the ears of Pope Pius XI, and it is said that he decided that it had undoubtably been a miracle.

Saved by the Bell

The following true story, which happened in the early 1970s, suggests that some benevolent force intervened to save scores of schoolchildren from death and serious injury.

One wintry morning in 1973, hundreds of children poured through the gates of St Anne's Roman Catholic Primary School in the Edge Hill district of Liverpool, quite unaware of the strange event that lay ahead. The road outside, Overbury Street, was coated with sheets of black ice and the grey heavy skies were laden with snow. Cars slid uncontrollably about as they passed the school, and the children gleefully trudged their way to the school playground, building snowmen and hurling snowballs at each other along the way.

Soon after nine o'clock the children filtered through the corridors from the assembly hall to their classrooms. As the morning drew to a close, the snowfall was relentless and caused the cancellation of playtime. Grumbling restlessly, the frustrated children were led once more into the assembly hall and shown faded cartoons on an old projector.

The morning lessons always ended for lunch at 11.30am, so at that time one of the prefects was sent down to the headmaster's office to press the button which activated all the electric bells throughout the school. The sound of these bells was eagerly awaited by the pupils, who were now desperate to get outdoors into the thick and tempting snow, before going home, or to the dining room for school dinners. But for some curious reason, the bells did not ring. One of the teachers glanced at his watch and saw that the time was almost 11.35am. Concerned about the delay, he went down to the headmaster's office and saw that the headmaster was pressing the bell button repeatedly.

"You must have broken it," he snapped, scolding the sulking prefect.

"I haven't, sir," he protested.

"What's the matter?" asked the teacher as he walked into the office.

"The bells won't ring," complained the headmaster, still rapidly pressing the button set into the wall.

The headmaster's secretary came in on hearing raised voices and suggested an alternative solution to the problem.

"There's an auxiliary back-up switch in the storeroom next door that rings the bells," she smiled.

With time ticking away, the headmaster, teacher and the prefect all went next door and located a small lever that was housed inside a box mounted on the wall. The headmaster pulled this lever, but still the bells would not ring.

"Damn!" he shouted with rising annoyance. He shook his head and turned to the prefect. "Right, you'll have to go to each class and tell them it's the lunch break."

As the prefect sulkily turned to leave the storeroom, there was a terrible crashing noise that literally shook the foundations of the school. The headmaster, the teacher and the secretary rushed outside to see what on earth was going on. The scene outside was one of complete devastation. Two enormous juggernauts, which had been on their way to Waterworths' fruit warehouse round the corner, had collided with each other on the black ice; they had smashed into the playground through the school gates. One of the immense juggernauts had actually turned over and flattened an entire section of the school railings, but luckily the drivers of both vehicles escaped with only minor cuts and bruises.

However, the headmaster and the teacher looked at each other with silent recognition of the disaster which had been so narrowly missed. If the lunchtime bell had rung out, scores of children would have been milling about at the exact scene of the lorry crash, and certainly many of them would have been killed. In other words, the schoolchildren had literally been saved by the bell.

As a safety test, later on that day, the headmaster again tried out the scholl's electric bells. He depressed the button and all the bells rang out simultaneously; the system was working perfectly, so why had the bell not worked at 11.30 that morning?

An electrician examined the button and the wiring and confessed that he could not explain why the bells had failed to ring out on that fateful wintry morning. Was it just some weird coincidence, or did someone 'up there' intervene to prevent a tragedy?

The Boy in the Red Tee-shirt

In November 1992, a 27-year-old woman named Lesley was abandoned by her partner of five years. A selfish rogue, he deserted her and their seven-year-old son, Alan, and moved down to London, apparently wanting to make a fresh start.

Alan was an inquisitive young lad and he wanted to know the reasons behind his father's absence in great depth. His heartbroken mother tried to explain to him that his father had found another person whom he loved more than her, to which little Alan had responded by innocently asking why, and suggesting that his mother should tell him to come home and they would give him his favourite ice-cream. Lesley's heart burned with sorrow. How could she explain to Alan that his daddy would not be coming back?

She did the best she could to get on with what was left of her life. A dedicated single mother, she ensured that Alan never wanted for anything. The love that he had lost from his absent father was more than compensated for by his mother's constant affection.

Alan was a very hyperactive child and Lesley used to call him the 'little dynamo' because he was so full of energy. One day she returned from the shops carrying a red tee-shirt for him. She hugged him and joked:

"I was told to make you wear something red like a fire engine so people can see you coming. You move too fast."

Alan giggled and raced into the garden, imitating the sirens of a fire engine.

In 1993, Leslie took Alan to the doctor because of what she thought was a simple ear infection. She was shocked to hear the doctor ask her to take her son to see a specialist at the Royal Liverpool Teaching Hospital.

"But why?" Lesley asked, as a heavy ball of fear grew in the pit of her stomach.

"Don't worry," said the doctor, trying to allay her fears with a stock smile, "I just want a specialist to check something, so we can be sure of … er … something."

Lesley took little Alan to the hospital and the specialist did discover something that absolutely devastated her: Alan had leukemia.

The spritely little dynamo gradually became too weak even to play. His health deteriorated over the months and Lesley was warned to expect the worst and prepare for the end. The last days were tortuous, although the neighbours helped a great deal, and Lesley's mother and sister did everything they could to ease the pain. One afternoon, Lesley asked to be alone with her son. She was holding Alan in her arms, gently rocking him, when the boy looked up at her and asked in a frail, strained voice, "Will I go to Heaven mummy?"

Lesley almost choked as she gave her reply.

"Of course, son," she whispered.

"Will you come to Heaven with me?" he asked, as tears began to stream down Lesley's face. She could only nod. Alan, though very weak, smiled when he saw this.

"When you get to Heaven, I'll have my red tee-shirt on, so you can see me straight away, mum."

Alan gently turned to his mother and just managed a faint kiss, before passing away.

Naturally, it took Lesley years to recover from the loss of her beloved son. Her life carried on emptily, until August 1995, when she met a man named Mike. She soon realised that she had at last found her soulmate. Lesley had been so hurt by the experience of losing her son, that she decided not to tell Mike about him, preferring to wait instead until she was ready to open up and purge all the sorrow from inside her.

About a month later, Mike was involved in a serious car crash in Wrexham and had to be cut from the vehicle. When he awoke in hospital, Lesley was at his bedside, desperately clutching his hand. Mike appeared to be fine and after he had caught his breath he related a very strange and thought-provoking encounter.

He explained that while he had been unconscious, he had seen a little boy who was surrounded by a halo of golden light. The cherubine boy had seemed to be standing right in front of him. He wore shorts and had on a bright red, short-sleeved tee-shirt. Mike's faced softened as he described how the boy's face had been remarkably beautiful and radiant. The child had said only a few words, "Tell Mummy I love her", before leaving him.

When Lesley heard this, her eyes brimmed with tears of both pain and elation. She felt that she was ready to share her cherished memories of her late son with Mike and so a few days later she presented a picture of Alan to him.

"That's him!" Mike exclaimed, with a baffled look, as he held the child's picture close to his eyes and smiled.

The couple's bond was intensified by the inexplicable experience, and Lesley and Mike were later married before moving to Leeds. Little Alan remained central to both their lives.

Tom Slemen welcomes details of ghostly experiences and unexplained phenomena. He can be contacted by email at: tomslemen@hotmail.com

Other Bluecoat Press books by Tom Slemen
Haunted Liverpool 1
Haunted Liverpool 2
Haunted Liverpool 3
Haunted Liverpool 4
Haunted Cheshire